D1546403

Feed the Tiger, Free the Dragon

Feed the Tiger, Free the Dragon

CREATE THE PASSION, FREEDOM, AND
RESPECT YOU DESERVE

Gillian Harper

GREENLEAF
BOOK GROUP PRESS

This book is intended as a reference volume only. It is sold with the understanding that the publisher and author are not engaged in rendering any professional services. The information given here is designed to help you make informed decisions. If you suspect that you have a problem that might require professional treatment or advice, you should seek competent help.

Published by Greenleaf Book Group Press
Austin, Texas
www.gbgpress.com

Distributed by Greenleaf Book Group

For ordering information or special discounts for bulk purchases, please contact Greenleaf Book Group at PO Box 91869, Austin, TX 78709, 512.891.6100.

Design and composition by Greenleaf Book Group and Lindsay Starr
Cover design by Greenleaf Book Group and Lindsay Starr

Publisher's Cataloging-in-Publication data is available.

Print ISBN: 978-1-62634-964-3

eBook ISBN: 978-1-62634-965-0

Part of the Tree Neutral® program, which offsets the number of trees consumed in the production and printing of this book by taking proactive steps, such as planting trees in direct proportion to the number of trees used: www.treeneutral.com

TreeNeutral

Printed in the United States of America on acid-free paper

22 23 24 25 26 27   10 9 8 7 6 5 4 3 2 1

First Edition

CONTENTS

Introduction

This is not a book about infidelity. Infidelity just happens to be where this book needs to start.

It was a random Tuesday morning, and I had briefly borrowed my husband Peter's laptop to do a few things. (I assure you, I was not snooping on my husband. It had never occurred to me to snoop. We'd been happily married for seventeen years.)

I opened his Dropbox account, intending to log out of his and into my own, but before I could click away, I was confronted with what appeared to be a series of pornographic photos. My initial reaction, after surprise, was, *No big deal. We're grown-ups. There's nothing wrong with a little porn.* But as I scrolled, I couldn't help but notice that the photos were all of the same woman. And mixed in with the naked photos of her voluptuous body were photos of her having coffee, lying on the beach, shopping—"normal" photos. Photos you'd take of someone you cared for.

As my mind tried to process what I was seeing, Peter walked into the room. Cutting off whatever he was about to say, I turned the computer so that it faced him and asked, "What am I looking at?"

His face turned white. "I'm not seeing her anymore," he replied. "It's over."

But for us, that was when an unexpected journey began.

As one might expect, we immediately went to see a crisis therapist. (Well, not immediately. First, I threw my hot coffee in Peter's face and went into physical shock. But after that, we went to see a therapist.) I had a lot of questions. I'm sure you do too. Who was she? Did he love her? Were there others? How many?

The Journey Begins

With guidance from our therapist, we embarked on an "infidelity disclosure process," which was exactly as painful as it sounds. During that process Peter sent me a spreadsheet (yes, an Excel-fucking-spreadsheet) outlining the number of women, the date range of each affair, and other details I'd requested. It turned out, Peter hadn't just had one affair, but also many, many affairs over our seventeen years together. The most recent affair, the affair I had discovered, was a four-year affair with a woman in Australia that had ended less than twelve months earlier, when I was pregnant with our second daughter, Stella.

Needless to say, I was shattered. So I did what most people do: I met with lawyers.

An aggressive attorney told me that, in his experience, men like my husband do not change. Peter was a bad person and a bad father. I should immediately leave with the children, go directly to the bank, withdraw all of our money as leverage, and get ready to fight. This attorney said he was confident we would "win" because he "could tell I was a good person."

Yet as angry and upset as I was, I knew my husband was not a bad person or father, and I was not simply "good." There was no "winning" in this situation. For anyone. Especially for me.

The second attorney I consulted had different advice. She explained that in all her years in practice, she had never heard a woman say that she regretted taking her time and trying to make the relationship work. However, women who rushed divorces almost always said that they wished they had slowed down a little, because life after divorce was not as easy as they'd thought it would be, particularly when small children were involved. This attorney's recommendation was to make as few life-changing decisions as humanly possible for twelve months. She encouraged me to wait for the trauma to subside and for some healing to occur before I made any decisions about my—or my babies'—future.

It was going to be hard, but that was the advice I decided to follow: *No major changes for a year.*

The "Year of No Changes" Brings Changes

During that year, I became obsessed with learning everything I could about our situation. Early on in the process I read that "it takes two people to have a marriage, but it takes three people to have an affair," and that resonated with me deeply. What was my role in all of this? How had I contributed to everything that had happened? I was determined to acknowledge my own accountability as much as possible. I knew that I had played a critical role in the destruction of our marriage, and I needed to fully understand that role if I was going to avoid repeating the same mistakes, whether with Peter or with someone new.

So I read, watched, and listened. I met with multiple therapists, psychiatrists, psychics, and mediums. I took mushrooms. I fasted. I cried. I even got rhinoplasty and breast implants to make myself feel better. Oh yeah. Shit got extreme.

And then, about six months into my prescribed "year of no changes," my head finally stopped spinning. I stopped feeling sick. I could eat again, sleep again, and even laugh a little from time to time.

When I looked at Peter, I no longer felt disgusted; in fact, I felt a new sensation that I was not expecting to feel—I felt *desire*. Out of nowhere, I found myself wildly and feverishly attracted to Peter. It was raw, almost animalistic . . . and really fucking confusing.

I hadn't felt true desire for Peter in over a decade. We were many things to each other—business partners, best friends, co-parents, workout buddies, and travel companions—but we hadn't been passionate lovers for a really long time. Don't get me wrong, we still had a sex life (clearly, seeing as we made two babies), but it just wasn't all that exciting. We "got it done" every other week and that was that.

For the ten years prior to the earth-shattering discovery, whenever I had looked at Peter, all I'd been able to see was his flaky scalp, hairy nipples, and crowded bottom teeth. Yet all of a sudden I didn't notice any of that. For what felt like the first time, I was seeing Peter as the tall, handsome, independent, successful man he was. And while I knew that some of this desire was driven by an acute fear of loss, it also felt deeper than that. Energetic. Magnetic.

An Attractive Force

I became obsessed with trying to understand this new sexual chemistry. What was it? Could we keep it going after our trauma subsided? And if so, how? Sexy lingerie? Candles? A jazz flute? Then, out of nowhere, my sister-in-law sent me a link to a podcast. After listening to it, I stopped dead in my tracks and thought, *Wow. This is it. This is the explanation we've been missing.* When I shared the podcast with Peter, we both finally exhaled. This was what we had been searching for, the cornerstone that would help us to rebuild our marriage. *Polarity.*

Up to this point both Peter and I (and our therapists) had deeply studied and discussed the drivers of infidelity. We'd contemplated narcissism, entitlement, sex addiction and love addiction, and Peter even went to AA while I puzzled over love languages and Freud's "penis envy" theory. But nothing resonated with us the way that Polarity did. Together we embarked on a journey to learn everything we could about this little-known natural law, all in an effort to save our marriage and hold our family together.

According to the Law of Polarity, people with opposite sexual energy produce an attractive force between them, while people with the same energy produce a neutral or repulsive force. As the old saying goes, opposites attract. And the larger the energetic distance between two people, the greater the attraction.

As it turned out, our trauma had pushed Peter and me deep into our opposing energies, and Polarity was creating a powerful attractive force between us. It was this sexual tension that had been missing from our relationship for the past decade. And as I looked back at our journey together, it all started to make sense.

Dragons and Tigers

During this journey of exploration of "sexual energy," everywhere I turned, I ran into discussions of masculine and feminine energy (usually with any negative attributes associated with the feminine label). The use of these gendered terms was heavily weighted and outdated and distracted us instead of helping us. We wanted to feel empowered to be our authentic selves in our relationship, and we didn't want to be boxed in by traditional terms. Peter's and my needs and energies were different, but they were equal in power and complexity, neither superior nor inferior to the other.

The challenge was finding a way to talk about and explore those differences in a way that would allow us to move forward as equals. Drawing on the imagery often used with the yin and yang concepts from Taoism, I began using the labels "Tiger" (yin) and "Dragon" (yang) to describe our energetic traits.

Over the following years, being able to apply the concept of Dragons and Tigers allowed Peter and me to more fully understand and embrace our differences and—ironically—to use those differences, the Polarity, to draw us closer together.

It has not been an easy journey, but our relationship is now full of mutual love, desire, and respect.

Fortunately, you don't need to wait for something seismic or traumatic like an affair to create the positive tension of Polarity in a relationship. There are techniques you can use to actively and constructively push yourself *away* from your partner or push them *away* from you—and, yes, I mean "away"—in order to regain some of the tension that attracted you to each other in the first place. That's what we'll explore in the coming chapters of this book. By the end, you will be able to quickly and easily create Polarity in your relationship, just when you need it.

Plus, understanding the principles of Polarity won't just allow you to create more passion with your partner: It will also help you to improve other areas of your life, such as deepening your friendships, advancing your career, and healing old family wounds.

PART I

Polarity

Opposites Attract

Peter and I met in law school. At that time, he was a chill, partying, festival-going, surfer student. He was beautiful, loving, wild, and free. He wasn't all that serious about his studies, and he certainly had no idea what his career or life purpose should be. But he had a light that followed him around and sparkled in every room he entered. There are many names for that sparkle in many different cultures: In Taoism, they call it yin, which is often represented by the totem of the *Tiger*.

We couldn't have been more different. I was focused, purpose-driven, and highly competitive. I graduated with honors, was recruited by a national top three law firm, and was soon off on my way to conquer the world. That purpose-driven energy is often known as yang, which is represented by the totem of the *Dragon*.

Peter thought my Dragon energy was sassy, feisty, and sexy as hell. He was deeply drawn to my confidence and clarity of purpose, the same way I was attracted to his chill Tiger vibe and wild joie de vivre. Peter helped me to relax, laugh, and love, and I inspired him to live up to his fullest potential. We were, in essence, polar opposites.

While we'll do a deep dive into the difference between the Dragon and Tiger energies in the coming chapters, in their simplest form, here are the basics:

- *Dragon energy* is your "doing" energy. Your inner Dragon gets shit done. It's the part of you that is competitive and driven by purpose.

- *Tiger energy* is your "feeling" energy. Your inner Tiger uses intuition and sensitivity to feel and nurture the world around you. It's the part of you that is untethered, wild, and radiant.

Counterbalance

Within ourselves, we each have the ability to embody the Dragon, as well as the Tiger. Yet at any given time, we tend to embody one energy more than the other. I call this embodiment our *Dominant Energy*. We are either a dominant Tiger, balanced by a little Dragon, or we are a dominant Dragon, balanced by a little Tiger.

Fig. 1.1. Dominant Tiger.

Fig. 1.2. Dominant Dragon.

We need counterbalance in our energy to function and succeed. If we were all Dragon, we would be overly aggressive and cutthroat, whereas if we were all Tiger, we would be uncontrollably wild and unhinged. It's the balance of both energies that ensures we can remain in harmony with the world and each other. According to Taoism, that balance follows a 70:30 ratio: 70 percent of our energy is embodied by either the Tiger or the Dragon, and 30 percent by the other.

Whatever our Dominant Energy is at any given time, it attracts our energetic opposite. Together with a polar opposite partner, we feel complete, whole, "one." Whether you believe in the Garden of Eden or evolution, whether you ascribe to Plato, Islam, Taoism, or Hinduism, virtually every creation story you'll find points to a time when everything was "one" and then became broken into "two." We are generally familiar with the concept of being "incomplete" on our own, and we seem to be born with that knowledge.

When Peter and I met for the first time, I finally felt whole, as if my final puzzle piece was fitting into place. It was so natural when we were together—it felt balanced and beautiful. Being with him made me feel calm, happy, and deeply loved.

Fig. 1.3.

Then somewhere in our late twenties, Peter changed. After years of floating through life, he started to buckle down. He enrolled to get his master's in international taxation, and he studied hard and worked even harder. He became focused on his goals and eventually built a thriving international practice with offices in Los Angeles, New York City, Atlanta, Chicago, Singapore, Sydney, and London. At the same time, I was also an entrepreneur and COO running a successful franchise system that had over 200 locations across the United States and Canada. By our early thirties, Peter and I were both working eighty hours a week and traveling more than 150 days a year. We often chuckled with friends about how we had now merged into one person: I was a little more fun, and he was a lot more serious. Our personalities were now strangely similar.

Fig. 1.4. Peter and I looked like this.

In hindsight, I regret making light of our merger, because there was really nothing funny about it. At home, Peter had lost his sparkle. He was no longer my wild Tiger: He was a fire-breathing Dragon. Our energy together wasn't balanced anymore, but abrasive. We didn't *complete* each other anymore; rather, we now *competed with* each other. We were both focused, determined, and in a constant state of conflict, battling for control.

My driven Dragon energy was no longer sassy and sexy to Peter. Instead, it felt cold and detached. Rather than being inspired by my sense of direction and purpose, he was repulsed by it and instead craved a deep devotion and warm nurturing that I wasn't yet able to provide. He still loved me, but he felt that I was incapable of loving him the way that he now wanted to be loved. And so he sought that love outside our marriage.

Shifting Energies

While Peter's energetic evolution—from a dominant Tiger to a dominant Dragon—occurred slowly over a decade, my personal experience with the opposite shift in energy—from Dragon to Tiger—was far more abrupt. Following the birth of our first daughter, Ophelia, I felt a sudden and seismic shift. And for two years, I fought it tooth and nail.

The old, familiar Dragon voice in my head tried to tell me that nothing needed to change: I could remain an executive working at the same pace; keep my start-up side hustle; and utilize nannies, housekeepers, cleaners, and night nurses to carry on as before. After all, I had managed over 100 employees via effective delegation—what was delegating a few more tasks at home? And yet this new feeling was emanating from my heart and creating conflict: I really didn't want to delegate motherhood.

From the second I held Ophelia in my arms, that all-doing Dragon impulse started to be drowned out by a newfound desire to love, nourish, and nurture that caught me completely off guard. I knew this "love" was something many people experienced after having children, and I felt ashamed, because I had judged those people harshly. I had thought I was going to be different. Yet motherhood had pierced my thick Dragon skin, and those work-related issues that had motivated me yesterday now felt trivial and empty.

So eventually I stopped fighting my Tiger. I finally let go.

Many people experience these seismic shifts of their Dominant Energy after major life events or times of great stress or pleasure, like a birth, death, marriage, or trauma. Sometimes it's temporary, and sometimes it's permanent. Either way, just knowing that it's natural and normal can help ease the confusion and internal conflict between what was and what now is.

After I let go and embraced my inner Tiger, I became more intuitive, flexible, nurturing, and compassionate. I took more time to relax, nourish, and heal my body. I let myself *feel* again. And when I did, I started to feel a new sensation. I felt . . . happy.

Right up until the moment I opened Peter's laptop.

Creating Tension

The timing of our marriage breakdown was incredibly fortuitous. Peter had always assumed that if I ever discovered his infidelity, I would immediately walk away. To his surprise, I stayed. If I had discovered his infidelity when I was deeply in my Dragon energy, things might have been different. But I had shifted into my Tiger, and my all-feeling Tiger wanted to stay. It also wanted Peter to stay, to choose me, to choose our little family, and to work things out.

After a decade of indifference to Peter's attention, it was now all I wanted. The fact that I was still there, trying to work it through, shocked Peter. He could now see that I had changed and opened my heart, and he was both deeply encouraged and deeply drawn to my newfound Tiger.

Yes, we were broken. But we were also feverishly, desperately, frantically, relentlessly, and urgently drawn to each other. If passion required tension, we now had an abundance, and it was palpable.

The easiest way to understand Polarity in practice is to imagine the sexual tension in your relationship as an elastic band, with you and your partner holding opposite ends of that band. When you stand right next to each other, the elastic is limp and lifeless, just like your desire. But as you start to walk away from each other, you begin to create tension in the elastic band. My energetic shift into my Tiger, coupled with Peter's infidelity, like it or not, had sent us careening away from each other. That band connecting us was taut.

The first step to creating Polarity is to deeply understand the Dragon and the Tiger. Because to create Polarity, someone needs to be predominantly in their Dragon and someone needs to be in their Tiger.

CHAPTER 2

The Differences Between Dragons and Tigers

Dragons and Tigers are most distinguishable in three areas:

- What motivates them
- Where they place their priorities
- What brings them pleasure

Understanding these differences is necessary to creating a foundation for greater Polarity and fulfillment in a relationship. Let me explain.

Motivation: Freedom vs. Love

Dragons are motivated by *freedom*. Their mantra is some version of *"I will be happy when I am free."*

There are many forms of freedom and endless interpretations of what freedom means to a Dragon in any given moment. It may mean physical freedom to sail a boat, financial freedom to retire, sexual freedom to sleep with whomever they want, or even just freedom to watch TV. Freedom may also look like emancipation from some form of arbitrary or despotic control, like a partner's complaining, a boss's micromanagement, a lover's seduction, or a parent's expectations.

When I was living in my Dragon in my twenties, I thought that everything in my life, including Peter, was secondary to my quest for freedom. My freedom looked something like, *"I will be free and happy when I am successful with my business."* This was a big goal for a twenty-five-year-old girl living in Brisbane, Australia. But when it became clear that our business needed more scale than the Australian market could offer, I raised seed capital and booked my flights to LA. Peter and I had only been married for two years at that point, and I told him that I hoped he would come, but either way I was leaving in six weeks. Chasing my freedom was my priority.

At this stage in his career, Peter was a tax attorney. Tax laws are heavily jurisdictional, and they don't travel internationally particularly well. It was also 2009, so the US job market was looking pretty shitty. Nevertheless, Peter resigned from an enjoyable job with a great firm, packed his bags, and came with me to America.

While we sugarcoated it, the truth was that our move to America required Peter to take a step back in his career. And despite outwardly supporting me on my quest, he really wasn't okay with his sacrifice. Over time, and as he evolved into the Dragon he is today, Peter accumulated tremendous amounts of resentment for, in theory, having to repress his freedom. In a subconscious protest, he started to seek out other freedoms. He traveled extensively (free time), went on dangerous snowboarding adventures (physical freedom), had extramarital affairs (sexual freedom), and spent money frivolously (financial freedom), all in an attempt to reassert his own personal freedom. As we'll discuss later, these are all phantom freedoms, and they did not fulfill Peter in his quest for true freedom. But at the time, those were his only outlets, and boy did he use them.

While Dragons feel a burning desire for freedom, Tigers have an unquenchable thirst to be deeply *seen and loved*. They want to be understood and genuinely loved for the person they are. Tigers want to shower in love, brush their teeth with love, and then floss with it. There simply cannot be too much love.

Thus, the Tiger's mantra is some version of *"I will be happy when I am truly seen and loved,"* and, as an extension of that, Tigers also believe *"I will be happy when I find someone to give my deep and endless love to."*

Tigers will spend a great deal of time and money attempting to be seen and loved. Some efforts are more obvious than others. A Tiger may focus on their personal appearance or the appearance of their belongings, family members, or even pets *("My children are beautiful, my home is beautiful, my social media feed is beautiful, therefore I am beautiful")*. They may work on being seen through their career achievements, their personal sacrifices, or their commitment to a cause *("See me for the difference I am making")*. They may even try to be seen through their bad habits and rebellious behaviors *("See me and save me from myself")*.

Tigers also have a deep desire to truly see their partner and get to know their inner thoughts, their desires, and their childhood fears. They want to know what their partner is eating for breakfast, what it tastes like, and how it impacts their digestion. A Tiger wants to show their partner that their love has no boundaries, and the more they see and feel their partner, the more they can bathe them with their love.

After I discovered Peter's infidelity, my heart was broken, but I was also overcome by a desperate desire for Peter's love and attention. Despite my pain, I still wanted him to see me. To love me. To choose me. The former Career Dragon Gillian would have immediately sought both physical and emotional freedom from this relationship. I would have cut and run. No one was more surprised by my response than me. That is when I knew that I had officially shed my Dragon energy and was living in my dominant Tiger, because I didn't want freedom from Peter at all. In fact, in the days and nights following my discovery of his infidelity, I wanted him to be around. Don't get me wrong. I was furious, confused, and crushed. But I knew I didn't want him to leave. I wanted him in bed with me. To hold me. To see me and love me.

I started to wear makeup and do my hair on the daily. I prioritized my body and fitness, and I scheduled all of those "self-improvement" projects that I had delayed for years. I fixed my teeth, my hair, and my sagging post-baby boobs, and I upgraded my wardrobe. I was a makeover movie montage. I wanted Peter to see me and desire me over anybody else. I was surprised by the idea that it *could have felt worse* if Peter had decided to leave, to choose someone else—to not only hurt me and lie to me, but also to then refuse to see me and reject me. But he didn't leave. He stayed and he saw me in my full, newly discovered Tiger heart (and body).

I wanted to see him too. I felt as though I hadn't "seen" him for years—especially with the revelation that he had managed to keep these deep secrets from me. I thought I knew Peter better than myself, but now I wondered if I really knew him at all.

And now I was seeing him as a fully independent (if not rebellious) Dragon. No longer an extension of me, but independent and free. Peter found my open heart irresistible, and I found his free spirit both captivating and confusingly desirable.

A Tiger who has an open heart and a deep yearning to be seen and loved is irresistible to a Dragon, particularly if that Tiger can also support and respect the Dragon's need for freedom (as long as that freedom doesn't result in pain or shame—more on that in Part II).

Similarly, the Tiger is drawn to a truly free Dragon—a Dragon who prioritizes their real freedom above all else—because the Tiger enjoys the process of competing for the Dragon's attention and discovering what it takes to be seen and then loved by them. It's the never-ending game of catch and release that the Tiger loves to play.

Priorities: Missions vs. Relationships

In addition to having different motivations (freedom vs. love), Tigers and Dragons also have completely different priorities in their daily lives.

Dragons are always on some form of "mission." The Dragon's mission might be getting a promotion, winning a gold medal, writing a screenplay, or buying a house. Whatever the mission is, the Dragon believes that through the success of their mission they will be free, and that is their top priority. It might be hard for a Dragon to admit to themselves (and their loved ones) that their missions are more important than their relationships, but they are. It doesn't mean that a Dragon won't have relationships or seek out love; it just means that these things are secondary to whatever happens to be their current mission.

After the kids were born, Peter sought freedom from financial stress, and his mission became to ensure financial security for our family by building his business and generating savings. Despite all of the work we did to save and strengthen our relationship, Peter admitted that he'd be willing to sacrifice it to keep his business. As much as he loved me, providing financially for his children was just more important. Similarly, upon asking whether he would choose love of his children over ensuring their financial needs were met, he answered that he would live without their love *if it meant they were secure.* He told me that it wasn't his job to have his children love him at every moment, but rather to protect them. That was his mission.

In direct contrast, a dominant Tiger will put successful personal relationships above all else. The Tiger doesn't live for a singular "mission," because Tiger energy is ethereal and goals can change in an instant based on new information and new relationships. Tigers feel free to change their minds and priorities at will. This doesn't mean a Tiger won't have goals—those goals are just secondary to their desire for the love and connection they gain through relationships.

When I asked myself the same question I had asked Peter— Would I give up my business to maintain his love and the love of our children?—my answer was categorically yes. While I love to have beautiful things, I feel that my daughters would much prefer my time, love, and empathy over anything that money might provide. It is most important to me that I am present with them, play with them, laugh with them, cuddle them, and kiss them endlessly to ensure that they feel my deep love for them. We can always work out the money.

Once you have an understanding and appreciation of your priorities, you will start to feel less conflicted in your choices. You will be able to live with more honesty and authenticity. There is nothing wrong with prioritizing your mission over your relationships or vice versa. The "right" choice all has to do with your Dominant Energy.

SIDEBAR: Testing Your Priorities

If you are still unsure whether your priorities indicate that you are more Dragon or Tiger, let's play out this work scenario:

You are working on an important project, and you have a hard and looming deadline. You are in your flow and hyper-focused on the task at hand. You are making great progress. Then your cell phone lights up. It's your best friend, who has texted you that they have an urgent problem, so could you please give them a call to discuss it? They need your help. Do you stop what you are doing and call your friend immediately? Or do you call them in a few hours when you have finished your work?

If you stopped what you were doing, you are most likely a Tiger. Your relationships are your primary driver. Just because you are a Tiger doesn't mean you can't be purpose-driven; it just means that your Dominant Energy is more focused on love.

If you decided to call your friend at lunch or after work when you were finished with your current task, you are more likely a Dragon. Your task/purpose is your primary driver. Being focused on your mission doesn't mean you don't value relationships; it means you don't value them as much as your mission.

Appreciating your own priorities, as well as those of your partner, can help reduce conflict in your relationship, because you can have a little more empathy for your respective competing interests. If your Dragon is distant, withdrawn, or inattentive, you can experience some level of comfort in understanding that, in all likelihood, this isn't about you at all. Your Dragon is on a mission. It's not that they don't love you, but you're not currently their top priority. (More on this in Part IV.)

Similarly, if your Tiger partner is suffocating you with their current wants and needs, know that, in all likelihood, they are not feeling seen and loved by you, and being seen and loved is their reason for existing. The more you ignore them, the more they will jump up and down trying to get your attention. (We'll circle back to this in Part V.)

Embracing these differences and learning to love the space between you and your partner will help you create more Polarity in your relationship and thereby more passion . . . which leads us to the third characteristic that distinguishes Tigers from Dragons: their polarized idea of pleasure.

Pleasure: Challenge vs. Connection

When it comes to experiencing pleasure, joy, and fun, the Dragon and the Tiger are light-years apart.

The Dragon derives pleasure from challenge and competition. Winning a challenge is like a mission-in-a-box for the Dragon. The idea of putting it all on the line is exhilarating and profoundly pleasurable. This desire for competition is why so many Dragons enjoy watching or participating in some form of sport. Sports are all about achieving freedom—breaking *free* of your opponent's tackle, succeeding at your *mission* to score, crossing a finish line first, or even beating a personal best in CrossFit. Playing the stock market, finishing a crossword, and collecting wine or figurines are other types of challenges that Dragons may find enjoyable.

Dragons enjoy challenge and competition so much that if they can't participate, they will try to experience it on TV, in a stadium, or through a simulation like a video game. You may even be surprised to find a Dragon enjoying an episode of *The Bachelor*, which, while it involves relationships, drama, and romance, is also a game with a clear mission and a winner.

In fact, a Tiger and a Dragon may watch *The Bachelor* together, but they are watching for different reasons. The Dragon is watching for the competition, while the Tiger is watching for the connection—specifically to *feel* the connection.

Tigers find immense pleasure in feeling a connection, and that feeling is best experienced through the senses. Activities like dance, yoga, meditation, swimming, and hiking all give the Tiger opportunities to connect with their mind, body, and nature. Even something as simple as a bunch of flowers on the dining room table can help a Tiger enjoy the connection with the beauty of the world. Of course, the ultimate connection for a Tiger involves other people. Tigers love connecting with fellow Tigers and sharing their passions like their food, plants, partners, pets, or children. Plus, sharing common interests helps the Tiger to feel connected with the world around them. The more sensory these interests are, the better.

While the Polarity of pleasure can play out in many different ways for Dragons and Tigers, their approach to sex is one of the most obvious. For the Dragon, having sex or masturbating is one more challenge with a very clear purpose—to be free of their overwhelming sense of desire. The Dragon will comfortably use pornographic material to assist, without craving any emotional attachment to the material itself. And while variety is nice, Dragons like to be efficient, so if something has worked with their sexual partner (or themselves) once, they will likely use it again and again to ensure the efficient and successful completion of the challenge. Dragons also tend to want to be in control of the mission to ensure it is successful, so they may be more active and dominating in the bedroom.

For the Tiger, sexual intimacy is an extension of their desire for connection and to be seen and loved—so seduction is important. Tigers will likely want to prepare for sex in advance, activating their senses via seductive clothing and grooming. When they feel attractive and desirable, the Tiger can relax and enjoy the experience. If the Tiger feels as though they are merely another tool assisting the Dragon in completing their challenge, they will not be deeply fulfilled by the experience and may even regret or resent their sexual encounter. Tigers ultimately see sex as an opportunity for intimacy and achieving a deeper connection with their partner. They want to use sex as a way of opening to the Dragon energy and welcoming the Dragon into their heart.

Vive la Différence

Mission, priorities, pleasure. The different ways Dragons and Tigers deal with these aspects of our lives can either ignite our own energy and the energy of our partners or be a source of tension and misunderstanding. It is critical to understand how to create the kind of Polarity that brings us together rather than pulls us apart, as I'll talk about more in the next chapter.

CHAPTER 3

Connecting with Your Dominant Energy

In the years leading up to the day that changed everything, Peter and I went through the usual ups and downs of married life. We reached what I think of now as an unsatisfying plateau, where everything was okay but the passionate moments in our lives were few and far between.

Once I realized that the foundation for Polarity is energetic distance, I could see that while living on our plateau, we were too often either competing to deal with the challenges in our lives in the same way (using the same energy style) or each moving uncomfortably away from our preferred energy.

We all contain both the Dragon and the Tiger, so we can enjoy both freedom and love, missions and relationships, as well as challenge and connection. But you will likely feel drawn to one more than the other. To create energetic space, it is important that you know what your Dominant Energy is, as well as that of your partner. Only once you know your starting point can you lean into your energy and push your partner into theirs. So to create Polarity you need to identify your Dominant Energy.

What Is Your Dominant Energy?

Perhaps you have already identified your Dominant Energy based on the discussion in the previous chapter. Are you more drawn to freedom or love? Do you sometimes ignore people in order to complete a task or mission? Or vice versa? Do you thrive on challenges or get more satisfaction from making connections?

If those concepts don't yet resonate with you, here's a quick, simple way I found that may help you to try to determine your Dominant Energy: Look at your recurring entertainment choices. In your down time, would you prefer to watch content centered on love and relationships, like *Sex and the City*, *Friends*, *Seinfeld*, and "romance/drama" movies? Or would you prefer to watch content centered on missions and competition, like ESPN, *Survivor*, and action/sci-fi movies? This is where many popular TV shows and movies really excel: The best ones manage to intertwine an action-packed challenge story with deep relationship-based subplots. This ensures there is something there for both the Tiger and the Dragon. *Game of Thrones* is a good example: It was the ultimate competition story jam-packed with love and loyalty subplots. *Gladiator*, *Sons of Anarchy*, and *The Sopranos* all did this well, too.

While entertainment choices can help us gather insights into our subconscious Dominant Energy, I want to caution against over-simplifying or trivializing the complexity of energy identification. Identifying a Dominant Energy can be challenging. After all, our energy composition changes every day based on where we are, who we are with, and what we are doing. We can also experience seismic shifts of our Dominant Energy after major life events or times of great stress or pleasure (like I did after Ophelia's birth).

Reading this, you may know immediately at the core of your being that you are a dominant Dragon, motivated by freedom, driven by clarity, and enthralled by a challenge. Similarly, you might immediately recognize yourself as a dominant Tiger, deeply motivated by love and a desire to be seen and feel connected.

But it's not always that straightforward.

Society's Dragon Bias

We can hardly ignore the fact that our career-focused, consumer-driven, capitalist culture glorifies and worships the energy of the Dragon. After all, the Dragon is purpose-driven, focused, and competitive. The Dragon gets shit done—and Western culture is all about doing.

From a very young age, we are encouraged (and often pressured) to lean into our Dragon energy. I was no exception. Time and time again, my family and society rewarded me for embracing my inner Dragon and, as a result, I spent such extended periods of time in that energy that I came to believe it was my natural state of being. I thought I was and always would be a Dragon.

Unless our careers require embodying Tiger energy—like in a creative industry or nurturing specialty—most of us spend a lot of our life operating from our Dragon energy in order to get work done. Business apps on our personal smartphones and work-from-home setups in our houses mean that there are no longer any clear work boundaries. When we bring our work into our home, we also bring that Dragon energy with us, and that blurs the energy lines considerably. It makes it difficult to determine whether we are *dominant* Dragons or just being dominated *by* our Dragon.

It isn't just careers that require our Dragon energy, either. Many people incorrectly assume that parenting and homemaking require nurturing Tiger energy, but for the most part, we use our Dragon energy to get that work done, too. Parenting and running a household require a great amount of discipline, routine, and organization—all traits of a Dragon.

If your initial reaction so far has been "my Dominant Energy is definitely Dragon," I would encourage you to open your mind and heart before you settle on that determination once and for all. We are so plugged into a society that rewards Dragon energy that it is sometimes hard to understand what truly motivates us, what our priorities are, and where we derive our deepest pleasure. It might take losing your primary relationship or loved one to realize how important that love and relationship is to you.

If you could keep your job and achieve your career goals, but the price you had to pay was the love of your partner, would you still do it? Or if you could run the perfect household, with color-coordinated task boards and a perfectly executed extracurricular schedule for the kids, but your children would hate you, would you still do it?

I spent so long in my Dragon energy that I started to believe it was my Dominant Energy. I believed that my purpose was more important than my relationships. If someone had asked me in my twenties whether I would choose my career goals or my husband, I might have answered "career" without thinking. However, upon testing that theory and almost actually losing my husband, it turns out that my younger self's impulsive answer would have been wrong. In the end, I chose love first. I genuinely felt—and still feel—that nothing was worth losing my marriage.

If you are still unsure about your Dominant Energy, or that of your partner, don't worry. Parts II and III will provide much more detail to help you work it out.

Pushing into Opposing Energies

For the majority of people, when you strip back the conditioned layers to finally reveal your Dominant Energy, you will likely notice that you and your partner are already polarized. We naturally gravitate toward our opposite energy—it's the Law of Polarity in action. Of course, this Polarity might not be obvious; over time, you both may have shifted, or you may have spent so much time together that you've become energetically similar, the way two magnets rubbed together depolarize. Yet deep at your core, when you are apart and fully energized, your natural states will likely be opposing.

The tools in the following chapters are designed to help you push yourself and your partner deeper into your respective opposing energies in order to create more space and more desire between you. The greatest attraction with your partner will be achieved through creating the greatest distance between your energies.

While the ideal scenario is for each partner to go deep into their own Dominant Energy and help their partner to do the same, you don't need to wait for your partner to get on board in order to get started. In fact, you don't need a partner at all. If you aren't currently in a relationship, you can use these chapters to learn how to nourish your own Dominant Energy, which will help you to better identify and attract the right energetic match. If you are in a relationship, there's a good chance that your partner will never read this book or take any interest in the topic. Don't worry: You can still go deeper into your own Dominant Energy, and you can help your partner to go deeper into theirs. Even if they don't know what you are doing, they will feel the difference—and that's what this is all about.

Taking the time to understand your own Dominant Energy won't just allow you to create more passion with your partner, but it will also help you to improve communication and reduce daily conflict.

It can also assist you in deepening your friendships, improving your career, and healing old family wounds. There's more about that in the later chapters of this book.

Now it's time to do a deep dive into the psyche of the Dragon and the Tiger. It's time to "Free the Dragon" and "Feel the Tiger," which are the subjects of Parts II and III.

PART I
ACTION STEPS

Exploring Your Energy

Here are three things to consider before moving on to Part II:

- With the knowledge that we embody one energy more than the other, which energy is your Dominant Energy? Are you a Tiger or a Dragon?

- If you have a partner, take a moment to consider their Dominant Energy: Are they a Tiger or a Dragon?

- Now, simply consider (pretending your partner doesn't exist, if you have one) what energy you are deeply attracted to.

PART II

Free the Dragon

In pretty much every fantasy story involving a dragon, the dragon is at some point feared, shackled, and locked in a cave. And yet, if Smaug (*Lord of the Rings*) and Drogon (*Game of Thrones*) have taught us anything, it's that no pesky human-forged chains can really imprison a badass fucking dragon.

That's right, Dragons, it's time to break free. It's time to own your inner Dragon, to stop apologizing for being different, and to go even deeper into your dominance. Not only will unshackling your deep Dragon energy help you be more desirable to your Tiger; it will also help you live a more authentic and meaningful existence. A life where you can experience freedom and purpose. A life worthy of your own deep respect.

First things first: Let's address that burning desire in your chest to be "free." What freedoms are you chasing right now? Are they financial? Will you finally be happy when your private jet flies you to freedom? Perhaps you'll finally be happy when you are free of your boss's micromanagement or free of those excess pounds you're carrying around.

It may not be easy to pinpoint the precise freedom that drives you because, like many Dragons, over time you probably learned to silence and sacrifice your desire for freedom for the perceived greater good of those you care for. Conversely, if you didn't learn to curb your desire, you likely soon discovered that achieving your idea of "freedom" didn't really satisfy you in a meaningful way. Any happiness felt after achieving freedom was probably fleeting and followed by a sense of emptiness and loneliness (until you found another freedom to chase . . . and another . . . and another).

Peter continued to chase sexual freedom while we were married. He believed that would make him happy, but when the reality of living out his freedom finally collided with the reality of our monogamous marriage, he realized he had merely stolen from tomorrow's happiness and was now paying the price of deep regret, shame, and sadness.[1] If the way in which a Dragon chases their freedom requires them to hurt others or act contrary to their personal values and beliefs, a very brief moment of joy will almost always be followed by a spiral of self-loathing.

All of these emotions surrounding your quest for freedom are very real; however, the "freedoms" being chased are not. Physical freedom, sexual freedom, financial freedom, freedom from time pressure, freedom from control—these are all ultimately illusions and distractions, which is why any joy they manage to deliver is so fleeting and shallow. They are *phantom freedoms*. Chasing them is no different from a greyhound chasing a rabbit at the dog track: The greyhound might catch the rabbit, but then what?

For a Dragon to find *real* happiness, they have to find *real* freedom. Soul-quenching freedom. Happiness-delivering freedom.

A Dragon will find real freedom when they can learn to escape the pain of their ego, self-doubt, and judgment. A Dragon will find real happiness when they find the real freedom that exists in the infinite of the moment.

Hang on. Hold up. "Find real freedom in the infinite of the moment" sounds a lot like enlightenment. Couldn't it be something easier than fucking enlightenment?

Okay, yes, enlightenment is the ultimate end game . . . but for us challenged souls just trying to tie our shoelaces, we need a more reasonable starting place.

Dragons can start to make strides toward their *real* freedom by learning to conquer the harsh criticism of their ego—and nothing silences self-doubt like *self-respect*. When a Dragon finds their self-respect, their life becomes grounded in pride. Because when you respect yourself (and when you feel your partner respects you), that respect provides much-needed relief to the burning in

---

1 Quick side note: In this chapter (and the coming chapters) you will notice that I will speak "for" Peter from time to time. He's my Dragon partner in crime, after all. Just know that he has indeed consented to this in advance.

your chest to be free. There is freedom in respect that you will learn to unlock in the following chapters. And it all starts with you identifying a meaningful and challenging purpose and fully owning your decisions.

CHAPTER 4

Dragons Thrive with Purpose

When Peter's infidelity was discovered, he was overcome by an intense fear of losing me and the kids. But he found a purpose for the immediate future: to keep his family together. Yet given that his seventeen years of infidelity were now out of the bag, that felt almost impossible. He didn't know how he would do it or if he could. But he knew that even though he had to live with the shame of his infidelity, he could not live with the shame of not trying to atone. Everything he now did, every mission, every decision, would be in support of his purpose.

Once he had a clear purpose driven by a healthy dose of fear, Peter was able to align all of his actions and decisions behind it. He had to be a better, more engaged, and present father; he had to do deep personal work through therapy; he had to be accountable, supportive, and receptive to every emotional fireball I threw at him; and he needed to turn it all off when he was at work so that he could run his company and provide financial stability for our family. He felt that if he could do all of that and be the best version of himself, then I might stay and, in time, forgive him and love him again.

To his credit, Peter worked at this purpose for years and continues to work at it every day. He is now reveling in life at the edge of his capabilities, and he is the husband and father that I knew he could be. I have found respect for him, and he finally has found respect for himself. He is free from self-loathing and free from my criticism. Despite everything we went through, despite my emotional meltdowns, despite spending more time at home, at work, and with his kids, Peter now feels more freedom and more happiness than he has ever felt before.

Purpose Leads to Self-Respect

Unconsciously, Peter took the first step toward attaining self-respect—which is what Dragons need to quench their burning desire for freedom—by identifying a very clear *purpose*. When Dragons have a clearly identified purpose and are on track to achieve that purpose, their burning desire to chase phantom freedoms gives way to clarity and their reason for being. A Dragon pursuing "purpose" feels respected and becomes impervious to criticisms, nagging, and neediness. A Dragon focused on purpose feels *free*.

If you are a Dragon, it's highly probable that purpose is a topic you have instinctually considered at length. I was deeply drawn to this topic when I was living in my Dragon energy, and over the years I've read countless books that have promised to help me unlock my "life purpose."

Most Dragons want to be born with a card tucked into their swaddle that says something like this:

Name: Sam Hudson
Date of Birth: Nov. 15, 1979
Time of Birth: 1:28 a.m.
Birth Weight: 8 lbs. 4 oz
Life Purpose: To save the Great Barrier Reef from
the crown-of-thorns starfish

If only life were that simple. And for some people, it is. They just *know* what they are meant to do and are able to align their life accordingly. But that's not how it worked out for Peter. While he's smart, motivated, and capable, he never had that deep sense of "knowing." As a teen and through his early thirties, he knew when something *wasn't* his life purpose—that was always easy to identify. But he didn't feel a calling to circumnavigate the globe, solo free climb El Capitan, or prevent babies from having middle ear infections. He just felt rudderless, frustrated and drifted from one phantom freedom to the next.

Purposeless Dragons feel as if they will be free when they finally know what their true north is—that one lifelong purpose that will guide their journey through life. Only then will they be free from the pointless wandering, the constant questioning, and the void of the unknown. But not knowing your true north doesn't mean you can't map out some coordinates to get your journey started.

Choose "a" Purpose

For those Dragons who feel a little lost in their search, try to let go of the idea that you only have one meaningful, momentous life purpose. Instead, replace it with "a" purpose. Because your life purpose can and will change over time, it will evolve as you do, so stop *chasing* that perfect purpose and start *living* a current purpose today.

It doesn't matter how trivial the purpose may seem, but it needs to be a purpose you believe in, and it has to be large enough to align missions behind it (more on that in a minute). It can come from any area of your life: money, career, family, intimacy, health, or community. You might decide your purpose is to run a marathon, get a master's degree, mentor a kid, fly a plane, or learn to play the guitar.

Having "a" purpose that you are committed to, above all else, will provide your life with much-needed grounding, direction, and focus. The tasks needed to achieve a purpose—what I call *missions*—will be easier to identify, decisions will be easier to make, and your life will be smoother and more satisfying. There is freedom in that focus. Moreover, any achievements made in service of your purpose will not only have deeper meaning, but they will also contribute to your sense of self-respect, making you feel grounded and strong in your Dragon energy.

You will also find that your depth and focus will act as magnets, attracting and evoking Tiger energy. The wild, untethered Tiger will be drawn to your stability and tenacity. Nothing is more attractive to the Tiger than a Dragon who has clarity of purpose and who is pushing themselves to the edge of their potential . . . which leads me to the second step of choosing a purpose: Make sure it pushes you to find your edge.

Find Your Edge

When choosing a purpose, you need to ensure that it's challenging enough to push you to your *edge of potential*. If your purpose is too shallow and fails to challenge you, your mind will wander and struggle to stay focused, and you will start to chase phantom freedoms once again.

Let's say your current purpose is to "buy a home and create a stable environment for your family." For some people, that purpose may not push them to the edge of their potential. Perhaps their parents and grandparents always modeled stability and home ownership for them, even agreeing to guarantee a mortgage and help with their deposit. For that person, home ownership is something inevitable; it's not a stretch. But for you, that purpose might feel barely attainable. Perhaps no one in your immediate family has ever owned a home or had job security or stability. You may need to start with a series of missions, such as getting a job (or a better job), furthering your education, improving your credit score, accumulating savings, and finding the right bank to fund you. Whatever it is, the purpose should stretch *you* to *your* edge. Forget everyone else.

You'll know that you are pushing yourself to your edge because the purpose will evoke a sense of fear. In this way, fear will be your guide in determining if your purpose is challenging enough. Perhaps you fear that your purpose is going to take a lot of time, money, and energy, or perhaps you fear that your purpose is beyond your capabilities. Whatever the fear is, listen to it and be guided by it. If you aren't feeling any sense of fear, you aren't challenging yourself enough.

Ultimately, striving for a purpose is not about whether you achieve that purpose or not. It's about the deep self-respect that flows from knowing you genuinely pushed yourself to the very limit of your own potential. Even though Peter developed his purpose of "keeping his family together," I could have easily and justifiably left him. And if I had, he would have been deeply disappointed, but he also would have known that he did everything in his power to change my mind. He would know in his heart that he put it all out there and would never have to wonder whether he could have done more to make me stay.

There is no freedom in the wondering. If you have a purpose that pushes you just beyond your limit and you fail, you will respect yourself for trying and you will find a form of happiness, because you will finally have found your edge. And when you are living at your edge, not only will you respect yourself, but those around you will also see that you are giving the world everything you have, and they will deeply respect you for that.

Check Your Edge with Other Dragons

Finding your edge is not without its challenges. Often it's easier for others to see your potential (and the edge of your potential) than it is for you to see your own. And there is nothing more frustrating to those around you than to watch a Dragon with awesome potential just floating through life, refusing to live at their limit. Or, equally as frustrating, to watch a Dragon live so far beyond their limit that they are wasting their time and energy on a complete and utter delusion of grandeur. We all have "that friend" who is going to be a billionaire with their next big idea, despite having no capital to set it up, no networks to raise money—not even an investment deck. It's hard to respect that friend because it is clear their life choices, purpose, and reality are not aligned.

Before going all in on your purpose, a sanity check is a good idea. In order to *really* achieve your purpose, you may need to completely blow up your current existence. You may need to quit your job, move cities, sell everything you own, leave your partner, change your friends, or cut off a destructive family member. But you don't want to make these dramatic changes unless achieving your purpose is within the realm of possibility. Your purpose should be a stretch—yes, it should be fear-inducing—but it should also still be possible. So once you have your purpose in mind, be sure to run it up the flagpole first . . . and ensure you're discerning as to whom you ask.

If you are in a relationship with a dominant Tiger, you will likely want to ask them for their thoughts, and you should—you are in a relationship, and communication is important. But keep in mind that Tigers are primarily motivated by relationships and love. If a Tiger thinks your purpose will take away from your commitment to the relationship and hinder your ability to see them and love them, they might react negatively to your plan (even if they don't mean to!). Alternatively, they may be so loving and supportive that they tell you what they think you want to hear, rather than what you need to hear, and blindly follow you off your edge into a purpose that is far beyond your potential. That's not helpful, either.

A good sanity check should come from a fellow Dragon. Dragons will appreciate your need for freedom, purpose, and respect. They will relate to the desire to challenge yourself. And because Dragon friends are less concerned about being "seen and loved" by you, they will be more candid with you than a Tiger. Still, don't ask any old unconscious, purposeless Dragon. Ask a Dragon you perceive as stronger or more successful than you in some way, and only ask a Dragon who you know is currently facing their own fears and living at their own edge. These are the Dragons you can respect and trust. Dragons of this kind will tell you how they see it, offer you specific actions to take, and give you the support necessary to live to your potential.

A Peer Group of Dragons

One of the powerful practices Peter uses is a support group called Entrepreneurs Organization (EO). In his "forum" he has six other successful Dragon entrepreneurs who meet to share their

continued

purpose, missions, challenges, and successes. They spend half of their time working on their businesses, and the rest of the time is spent on personal growth. They deeply respect one another, but they are also extremely candid and don't hold back on calling bullshit when they see it. When Peter shared his infidelity and current purpose with them, not only did they encourage him to try to save his relationship, but they also continued to support him when it all felt hopeless. They shared their own experiences, advice, and guidance, which helped him to strive forward and push himself beyond what he thought was possible.

In addition to checking your purpose and your edge with those Dragons you respect, a useful self-check is to see if those Dragons are also asking you for your guidance and feedback. If a fellow Dragon does not believe you are living up to your potential, or at least trying, they will not seek your guidance because they do not respect you. They might like you a lot, and they might think you are great company and fun to be around, but they won't look to you for insights on issues of substance. So if no one's asking you for your input, that's a good indication that you're not living at your edge.

Nothing makes Peter feel more respected and valued than when one of his EO Dragons calls him for his counsel. Ironically, he is now the go-to guy for relationship advice. He feels validated and respected when his friends reach out to him for guidance. He uses those moments to reassure himself that he is on track with his life and living his purpose fully. In these moments he feels pretty darn *free*.

Shed Your Skin

It is inevitable that over time, as you continue to challenge yourself, you will grow and evolve. You will complete your missions and, eventually, outgrow your current purpose. And when you do, like all reptiles, you will need to shed your skin.

You'll know when it's time. Maybe you accomplished your purpose, or perhaps your purpose isn't interesting anymore. It may even suddenly seem juvenile, silly, or foolish. Or your purpose and missions may no longer push you to your edge because they're just too easy. Whenever you stop feeling fearful and challenged, you know it's time to grow. You may not consciously realize that you have outgrown your purpose, but unrest is a telltale sign. Just before a reptile sheds their skin, they get irritable, stressed, and skittish. They act a little odd, and they don't want to be handled. Likewise, you may unconsciously start to feel restless, frustrated, stressed, and irritable, and you may crave physical space and time alone. When that happens, take a moment to acknowledge how you are feeling. If you have indeed outgrown your purpose, then consciously let it go. Shed it.

Sometimes, after shedding your old purpose, you will immediately identify a new purpose and set off with clarity on your next mission. Sometimes you will not. You may need to take some time for solitude while you reflect on your life to date and search for that new purpose to anchor you. Just know that there is only one direction for you: forward. You cannot go back to the person you were before; you have outgrown that person. A snake would never try to wiggle back into an old skin that it has shed, and neither should you.

While you are in transit from one purpose to the next, know that you will likely feel uncomfortable, lost, and even a little depressed. Your time in solitude may make you feel proud of your achievements, but it may also make you question your worth, your life's work, and your potential. During this process, you will more than likely be tempted to chase a few phantom freedom rabbits around the racetrack. If you can, resist the temptation and, instead, be intentional and conscious of where you are in your purpose progression. Be sure to take a little Dragon time (see Chapter 6), by checking in with other Dragons whom you trust and respect and who inspire you. They will help you in your transition.

The process of growing into a new purpose will likely get a little easier each time you do it, as you will become more conscious of the process. Know that with each new achievement and purpose, you will reach a new depth of consciousness and creep closer to that deeper purpose and meaning you are searching for. You will get closer to finding the real freedom where your own deep self-respect exists—in the infinite of the moment.

CHAPTER 5

The Decisions That Shape Your Dragon Path

After our marriage blew up and Peter had clearly articulated his purpose to "keep his family together," he was then able to align his missions behind that. Missions are, essentially, smaller, more actionable purposes. Peter's missions were to be a present and loving father and an exceptional financial provider, and he also wanted to make himself as attractive as possible (both mentally and physically) so that I would want to stay. In order to do all of that, he knew he could not fall into a pit of despair and self-loathing; he couldn't drink too much or run away from our problems. I didn't make it easy on him. I was throwing all sorts of emotional stuff at him (and some physical stuff), and it was hard for him to hold it all together.

But he knew if he was going to have a shot at his purpose, he needed to stay strong. So Peter made decisions that would keep him strong: He chose not to drink and to continue exercising every day, he hired both a personal therapist and a business coach, and he spent absolutely every spare moment he had with the kids and me. He was able to use his purpose and missions as a filter through which to make those decisions. This made it easier to say "no" to things that weren't aligned (like a night out with his buddies) and "yes" to the things that were (a pizza night with us, his girls).

Over time, those small decisions built a consistency of behavior that soothed me. Through the deep alignment of his purpose, missions, and decisions, we could rebuild our life together. And when Peter could see that I felt safe and secure in our marriage once more, he knew he was achieving his purpose. Only then, from that solid foundation, could he start to look at building and growing into another challenging purpose.

The same is true for all Dragons. Once you have a current purpose and it is clearly articulated, you can align your life in support of that purpose. Every mission you embark on needs to be in service of that purpose, and every decision you make should support your missions.

Unlock the Power of Your Decisions

Once you are clear about your *purpose*, the second stage of your Dragon development is to unlock the power of your *decisions*. The decisions you make every day—and the way in which you make them—play a critical role in your development as a Dragon. Not every single decision in your life will be relevant to your purpose or a mission—what color socks you wear probably has no bearing on your life purpose. Yet the mere practice of making your own decisions and then standing behind those decisions serves an important energetic purpose. The more decisions you make and own, the deeper you will push into your Dragon energy.

Decision-making can help a Dragon experience a true sense of accomplishment and self-respect. And despite what you may think, your Tiger partner loves it when you make decisions—it's incredibly attractive.

So this should be simple enough, right? Make decisions, reap the rewards. But decision-making can be more challenging than it first appears. Like most things, the devil (or should I say Dragon) is in the details.

Make Your Own Decisions

After we moved to America, I went about setting up my business as planned. I started to burn cash pretty fast and required significantly more capital than I had initially raised. Finally I asked Peter if we could personally invest our savings into the business. It was not an insignificant sum of money, and I wanted to ensure that using it this way wouldn't cause any problems in our marriage. After months of discussing and languishing—and despite the fact that Peter did not want to invest in the business—he finally said that if I believed in the business and I wanted to invest, he would not stand in the way. He did not want to be the reason I did not realize my dreams. So, I went ahead and invested our savings into the deal. All of it. It was a gamble—and like so many gambles, this one didn't quite pan out. When the business wasn't as successful as we had hoped, Peter became angry and immediately blamed me for our loss. He fell into a dark spiral of bitterness and resentment, to the point that he could barely look at me.

Eventually, those feelings he harbored against me passed and were replaced with feelings of shame and self-loathing—he was furious with himself for not actively making and owning such an important life decision. He realized that he had indeed made a decision, and that decision was to "delegate his decision."

Sometimes delegating a decision is perfectly acceptable, particularly if you don't really care about the outcome (for example, when ordering takeout). But if the decision is important, like investing all of your savings, and you have your own strong preference, then delegating your decision-making power can be disastrous.

If Peter had actively made the decision to say no to investing in my business, it would have been hard for me to hear, but the decision would have been his, and he would have felt self-respect for standing his ground. However, at that stage in our life, he wasn't ready to make his own decisions. He didn't have a defined purpose, and he wasn't on a mission; he was more comfortable living out a vicious cycle of delegation, blame, and victimhood. When you can blame someone else for your life path, you don't have to take personal accountability for your success or your failure. Even though there is no responsibility in walking that path, there is also no freedom. You are merely a passenger on someone else's journey.

Stand Behind Your Decisions

After learning the importance of determining his own path, Peter became the master of owning his own decisions—and the more he owned his decisions, the deeper he pushed into his Dragon energy, the more Polarity we created, and the more sexually attracted to him I became. Sometimes it was the small decisions that would be the sexiest, like when he would walk out wearing a T-shirt and shorts to go to dinner, and I would say, "You can't wear that; you need to go put on some pants." He would look me in the eye and say, "This is what I am wearing. If you don't like it, feel free to stay home." He would then go straight to the garage and start the car.

At first, I was left standing with my mouth open. Who was this person? The Peter of old might have questioned his own decision and turned around to go change into pants. That also would have made him feel like a child who couldn't dress himself instead of a fully functioning adult who can make that decision, as well as many more important decisions, every single day.

In reality, Peter's past self would still have been defiant, which would have led to a brief power struggle between us where I would roll my eyes, say something sarcastic, and passive-aggressively shame him into changing. Or, alternatively, we would have had a fight that would tarnish our entire evening because he would have felt belittled and I would have felt bewildered by his poor choice of pants.

Instead of taking the bait and rising to the challenge, Peter has now learned to laugh off my protests and simply refuse to engage. He stands by his decisions and roots himself deeply in his Dragon energy. Over time, the more he practiced and the more consistent he was, the less I tried to intervene. As this example shows, not only does consistently making and standing behind your own decisions lead to self-respect, but it also leads to a consistent pattern that the Tiger can trust and respect.

Before Peter started to consistently make and own his decisions, I didn't feel as though I could depend on him. If I couldn't depend on him to dress himself appropriately, how could I depend on him with other decisions, like driving the car or feeding the kids? Let alone major decisions like where we should live and how we should use our money. As Peter started to stand behind his decisions, I began to develop a deep respect for him as a fully independent, self-driving, pant-wearing, accountable Dragon. He was no longer just a passenger in our lives. He was charting our true north.

Change Your Mind

Having made a decision doesn't mean you can't change your mind. Dragon energy has a tendency to want to function linearly: to make a decision, draw a line under it, and then move on to the next decision. However, if you are presented with new and important information, take the time to consider the choice again. It's a brand-new decision, so don't be perturbed if your choice is different. As much as you wish it were, life just isn't linear. The important thing is that the decision continues to be yours.

If I had provided Peter with new information about our dinner date—let's say I forgot to mention to him that dinner was at the country club, and they have a strict pants policy—that would be a new decision. He could then stop, consider the new information, and make a new decision. He could still decide to wear his shorts to dinner, which might mean being turned away from the club, or he could choose to go inside and put on some pants. Changing into pants based on this new information is completely different from letting me choose what he is going to wear for the evening.

The distinction here is critical: "Changing your mind" is different from "having your mind changed." And there is nothing the Tiger loves more than to get you to change your mind—to *test* you. A Tiger will constantly and relentlessly test the Dragon to see if they will waver from their purpose, mission, and decisions. Testing comes in all forms: It might look like complaining, criticism, challenge, doubt, distraction, or undermining. It may be subtle or obvious, it may be conscious or subconscious, but one thing is for sure: Tiger testing is inevitable.

When I questioned Peter's decision to wear shorts to dinner, I was really testing his ability to make his own decisions and stand behind them. Because, as crazy as this sounds, by standing behind his decision to wear shorts, he is more likely to stand behind his decision to *love* me. Sounds crazy, right? But this is real.

Tigers will test you to see what it will take to get you to *change your mind*, because if you fail the test and change your mind, what is stopping you from changing your mind about loving them? Tigers want to relax deeply into their Tiger energy, but they can only do that when they feel safe and secure in your love, and that feeling of safety comes from feeling your resolve. When the Tiger cannot move you or manipulate you, the Tiger can then learn to trust your depth, your strength, and your stability.

Own the Outcome

Your depth and strength as a Dragon are fortified when you fully and personally own the outcomes of your decisions. That's fairly easy to do when the outcome is good; when things go well, you can revel in your achievement. The degree of happiness you feel when you succeed at something you chose to pursue is almost divine. It's *your* win. You get to bask fully in the glory. But owning decisions when the outcome is lousy is harder to master.

When a decision you have made has dire consequences, particularly when it hurts others, it is far less burdensome to place the ownership of the decision elsewhere—to blame someone for changing your mind or blame elements outside your control for the outcome. Yet your depth and strength come from standing firm and taking full accountability for the outcome, no matter how painful the consequences may be.

When I initially uncovered Peter's infidelity, his first involuntary response was to blame me. He tried to blame my disinterest in our sex life, my emasculating behaviors, my career choices, and my family. He had been playing those tapes in his mind for seventeen years, which made those arguments sound rational and reasonable. Yet when he finally spoke them out loud in the stark light of day, they landed false and hollow. He quickly realized that blame was not the path forward if we were going to make it through this crisis. The cycle of delegation, blame, and self-loathing in which he was stuck had started long before he met me. His path forward was to take ownership for his choices—both in the past and moving into the future—and to stand firmly in the consequences that flowed from those decisions, no matter how much they had hurt me. It was only when he stopped blaming me that we could start to heal and rebuild our life together.

When you own the outcome of your decisions, as challenging as this can be, you will feel power in your resolve and even get a glimpse of the infinite strength that exists within you. You are a Dragon, after all.

CHAPTER 6

Optimizing Your Dragon Time

You are now well on your way to pushing deeper into your Dragon. You're facing your fears, finding your edge, living with purpose, aligning your missions, making decisions, owning the outcomes, and passing tests from your Tiger. That's intense. (I didn't say it would be easy!)

In addition to all of that, it's important that you are also finding enough conscious time, whether alone or with your fellow Dragons, to recharge and ground your Dragon energy. This is specifically time to be free—time to find the infinite in the moment.

Time with Fellow Dragons

It is hard to sharpen your Dragon energy if you are spending a lot of time around Tiger energy, because unconsciously we emulate those around us. If you spend excessive time with Tigers, you will likely find your Dragon energy moving further toward the Tiger pole. Likewise, your Tiger partner will become more Dragon-like simply by spending long periods of time in your presence or in the presence of other Dragons. It might seem hard to take time apart—you've likely chosen your partner because you truly love their company—but if you spend too much time together, you will demagnetize, just like two magnets that rub up against each other. Instead, spend some time with fellow Dragons, and encourage your partner to spend more time with Tiger friends. This will recharge your Polarity by creating some space between you.

Peter's Entrepreneur Organization (EO) forum meets for a half day once a month, and each year they go on two weekend retreats and one longer international trip. It's not a huge amount of time, but when they are together, they make the most of it. On their international trips, they study and learn about the country and the culture they are visiting, they tour other successful international businesses, and they find time to learn more about themselves and one another. They expose their blind spots, both good and bad, and learn to hear hard truths by developing a thick skin for feedback and constructive criticism. Peter returns from his trips energized, deeply motivated, and squarely focused on his purpose.

Spending time with fellow Dragons will remind you of their natural inclination toward challenge and competition—a depth you also share. This will help to charge your Dragon energy. If you have somehow lost your way, Dragon time will help put you back on track with your purpose and will inspire you to push yourself a little harder and a little further.

In addition to supporting Peter through our trauma, the EO forum has helped him to face some of his other fears over the years, like his fear of public speaking. The members constantly challenge one another to live at the edge of their potential, to do better, and to be better. They also try to outperform one another. At one point they even had a fitness challenge where, over a six-month period, all of the members managed to get their body fat percentages below 15 percent. That's the power of spending conscious time with other Dragons and doing the work.

Yet in addition to prioritizing time with your fellow Dragons, it is also important that you prioritize a little time on your own.

Take Free Time

Small doses of conscious free time can help you to stoke the fire in your belly. Free time is when a Dragon takes time that is 100 percent obligation free. This is time where you can be free from earning money, looking after the kids, talking to your partner, pleasing your parents, or picking up your dog's poop.

For it to count, you need to truly own it, not steal it. Sneaking to a bar after work, zoning out when you are supposed to be talking to your partner, or disappearing for an extended period in the bathroom are all ways that Dragons steal time. But stolen time won't feed the fire in your belly the way conscious time ownership will—and the people in your life won't respect you for stealing time. Your decision to take free time is like any other decision: You need to stand behind it and own it, along with any consequences that follow. If you can define the time you are taking and acknowledge why you are taking it—even just thirty minutes a day—it will have far more meaning, power, and strength.

As challenging as it can be, try to use some of that free time for deep solitude. It's hard to listen to your fears and discover your purpose if you are being drowned and distracted by life's comforts. Find time to challenge yourself in the discomfort of your solitude. Deprive yourself of anything that can distract you from your own fear and malaise. Take time without the comforts of your daily routine that lubricate your day—time without television, news, your phone, music, a crossword, anything. Take time to be alone with your own consciousness. If you can meditate, great, but if not, just be alone while you ponder your own purpose. Be bored. Truly bored. Push through the uncomfortable feeling of that boredom to take a peak over the edge of your existence. This practice will help push you deeper into your Dragon.

Becoming a Mindful Dragon

If your thoughts and emotions are running wild, then your consciousness isn't free; it is bound and trapped by your mind. In your quest for ultimate happiness through freedom, a Dragon must also be free to find the infinite in the moment. Try using this Dragon-grounding technique to free your mind from wild thoughts and emotions:

Find a place to be still and alone.
Sit comfortably and close your eyes.
Now visualize your body. Notice how strong it is. Take three deep breaths and start to lengthen your spine.
Feel your entire body. Feel how long, straight, and strong your spine is. Feel how strong your thighs are and how strong your groin is. Take another deep breath and truly feel your strength.
Now visualize the base of your spine. You're a Dragon, so begin to see and feel that, extending from the base of your spine, you have a long, strong Dragon's tail. Feel your tail, feel its strength, feel it move. Now that you own your tail, imagine pushing your Dragon's tail deep into the earth. It is so long and strong that it can penetrate all the way to the center of the earth and coil itself around the molten lava at the earth's core. You are

now one with the earth and firmly anchored by its fiery center. You are grounded. You are strong.

Stay like that, coiled to the center of the earth, and take a deep, slow breath. As you inhale, visualize the fire from the earth's core traveling up your tail, into your groin, into your belly, and filling your lungs. Do it again, this time deeper. With each inhale the earth's magma travels up your tail and fills your entire body with fire and strength. Your body is now a fiery ball of power and energy.

Now take another deep, slow, fiery breath. This time, focus on the exhale. As you breathe out, imagine all of those thoughts that are trapped in your mind getting pushed out of your mouth in a fiery ball—all that fear, doubt, and insecurity. As you exhale, watch those thoughts leave your body in a fiery ball. Watch the fire leave your body and completely melt them away into ash and vapor. Watch the black smoke rise into the air and disappear.

Slowly uncoil your tail from the center of the earth. Coil your tail at your feet. Slowly, gradually, feel your body start to cool. Feel relief from the fire.

Be free, be grounded, be strong.

You can repeat that simple meditation anytime you feel your Dragon energy slipping. By completing this simple meditation, you will start to feel free and grounded. You may even notice that you will start to talk a little slower and a little deeper because your consciousness will be pulled closer to the fiery center of the earth. Try doing this activity just before you make passionate love to your partner, and feel the difference the grounded Dragon can make.

Welcome the Dragon Challenge

Living a deep Dragon existence is not without its challenges: Phantom freedoms will tempt you, Tigers will test you, and life will not let you develop in a straight line. All of this is certain. The good news is that Dragons love a challenge. Is there any greater or more rewarding challenge than trying to live an authentic and meaningful life? A life lived with purpose. A life worthy of your own deep respect.

Living Your Best Dragon Life

Dragons love efficiency, so here's a succinct action list to help you start living your best Dragon life today:

1. Stop chasing phantom freedoms. Instead, endeavor to find your *real* freedom by learning to escape the pain of your ego, self-doubt, and judgment. You can achieve this by building self-respect and earning respect from others. There is *real* freedom in respect.

2. Find self-respect by living your life with purpose. Forget the "perfect life purpose" and simply start living your life with "a" purpose. Your purpose should push you to the edge of your potential and instill a bit of fear in you. Align your daily missions and decisions behind that purpose.

3. Once you have achieved or outgrown your purpose, shed your skin and start again. Keep evolving.

4. Go deep into your Dragon by consistently making your own decisions and standing behind the outcomes.

5. Prioritize spending time with other Dragons you respect. They will challenge you, enliven you, help you check your purpose, and keep you on track once you've chosen what purpose to pursue.

6. Find time to challenge yourself in the discomfort of your solitude, even if it is just for thirty minutes each day. Be bored, uncomfortable, and ultimately free to find the infinite in the moment.

PART III

Feel the Tiger

I love watching tigers play with their handlers at the zoo. It's nothing short of mesmerizing, not simply because tigers are majestic and beautiful, but because of the sheer restraint they exhibit. I'm on the edge of my seat knowing that this wild, 500-pound creature could in an instant use any one of its abilities—its claws, teeth, speed, strength, or agility—to display its true power. And yet the tiger consistently exercises immense self-control.

Those imbued with Tiger energy will understand this feeling of restraint, of consistently holding back. Deep down you know that you have more power within you, lying dormant beneath the surface. You have more frustration to share, more anger to release, more pleasure to feel, more love to give, and more light to shine. So. Much. Fucking. More.

When you finally stop exercising so much restraint, when you learn to let go and to release that powerful Tiger energy, not only will you capture the attention and desire of the Dragon, but you will also finally experience a more fulfilling, untamed existence. A life worthy of your own open heart. A life where you can experience more *love*.

The dominant Tiger believes that it will finally be happy when it feels *enough* love. And the open Tiger heart constantly craves more. Be honest: Deep down, what love are you craving? Do you want more love from your parents? Your Instagram followers? The Michelin Guide food critic? Maybe you will finally be happy when people love your new haircut, or when your Beliebers start chasing you around the world and smothering you with their love.

Or perhaps you don't crave the love of 100 million followers—perhaps you're simply looking for the love of one special person. And when you capture the attention of "the one," when they look into your eyes and see your soul and everything you are, then, finally, you will experience deep, unstoppable love and that will make you happy. Or so you think.

That soulmate searcher? That was me. I believed that when I found my "person," I would finally be happy. And I did find Peter—a beautiful man who completed me, saw me, loved me. And I was happy . . . for a brief moment. Then I started to second-guess my decision. Would I be happier if I were with someone else?

The reality is that the fleeting moments of happiness we feel through the love and attention we receive from others just don't deeply nourish our souls. It's a Coca-Cola kind of happiness: a quick, bubbly, sweet-salty sugar rush followed by chronic dehydration.

A Tiger will feel real love when they can learn to overcome their desire for attention and external validation. A Tiger will feel real love when they feel the infinite love that is available in the present moment.

Hmm. As a Tiger who has spent her life chasing attention and external validation, I believe this sounds pretty close to impossible. But as I have learned, we can't let perfection be the enemy of progress. If you're like me and know this pursuit will be a struggle, fear not—I assure you we can still grow and edge our way toward feeling some real, authentic love and happiness.

And the first step in feeling more love is to feel more, period.

That's right, Tiger, it's time to stop holding back. Stop showing such restraint and *let go.* Because by releasing your frustration, pain, anger, and shame, by releasing your wildness and allowing your feelings to freely move through you, you create more space for your bliss, your pleasure, your real happiness and love. No longer caged, you are the beautiful, majestic Tiger sprinting through the savanna. And your freedom and power are captivating, inspiring . . . and magnetic.

Tiger energy is the free, open, emotive counterbalance to the structured Dragon. Where the Dragon pushes deep into their energy by focusing on their purpose, decisions, and respect, the Tiger expands their energy by letting go, surrendering to the moment, and feeling it all the way through to their pleasure.

So let's start there, with *feeling* a little more. In order to do that, you are going to have to stop showing so much restraint. Stop holding back. It's time to let go and feel it all.

CHAPTER 7

Break Open

When my daughters, Ophelia and Stella, were three and two, I was truly tested by their raw emotions. I found myself parenting them to back away from their feelings and their wildness. When I asked myself why I was doing that, it was clear that I didn't want them to misbehave in public because that would impact the way I was seen— as a bad mother, a mother who couldn't or wouldn't "control" her children, a mother who would allow her children to behave in a way that could disrupt someone else's quiet enjoyment of the moment. So I found myself trying to minimize and control their outbursts and mood swings. If the girls lost control of their emotions, I would send them to their room to "take a minute," "compose themselves," and "stop being ridiculous." Suddenly, I became aware that I was training them to suppress their feelings.

All of us, irrespective of who we are, are conscripted into some version of "Dragon Training" practically from the day we are born. Society subtly and consistently teaches us how to stoke the fire of our inner Dragon: how to *do*, how to *achieve*, how to live life with *purpose* and garner *respect*. Part of that training is also learning how to restrain our feelings and our wildness, because in the end, Dragons are all about getting shit done—and raw emotions aren't very conducive to efficiency. It's hard to meet a deadline, solve a problem, or win a medal if you are distracted by your pesky feelings. Do now, feel later (if you must).

In addition to strong emotions being highly distracting, we are made to believe that they are silly and even embarrassing. So we subtly learn to put up walls, hide away, and feel in the shadows. When we're dating, we are told to play it cool and tone down our excitement in case we scare our potential new lover away. If we are at work and need to cry, we go to the bathroom or hide in a cubicle, afraid of appearing weak or unhinged.

It gets worse for us Tigers. We started our lives with an open heart, just raw little bundles of joy. Then slowly and surely, as we shared our love with people, some of whom were reckless, hurtful, or cruel, we started to subconsciously withdraw. Our injured inner Tiger built itself an enclosure and retreated there to safety. In this strange scenario of Tiger Stockholm syndrome, we are both the captor and captive of our own feelings.

Meanwhile, society, instead of shining its light on our strange syndrome, naively reinforces our rhetoric, reassuring us that we were wise to build such a beautiful enclosure. Clever to stay caged.

Well, Tigers, it's time to stop listening to the bullshit. It's time to break free and break open. In order to do that, you are going to have to try to forget a few things . . . like your Dragon Training. It's time for some counterbalance. We've had plenty of training in how to "lean in" and *do* more. Now it's time to "lean in" and *feel* more. Because we'll never find our soul-quenching pleasure if we don't let ourselves feel.

Let the Tiger Rain Fall

When Dragons are faced with stress and trauma, Dragons do what Dragons do best: They hyper-focus on the issue in front of them, making the issue as small as possible, and then they pragmatically go about solving that particular problem. In a word, they *contract*. When Tigers are faced with the same stress and trauma, they instinctively want to do the opposite: They want to make the issue much bigger than it is. They *expand*.

As they expand, the issue confronting the Tiger becomes the immediate issue, yesterday's issue, and every marginally related issue they have ever had. All the little issues start to collect and condense onto one another, like droplets, and then, when the cloud of issues gets too big and heavy to carry, the issues release in a torrential downpour of *Tiger Rain*.

A lot of us try to avoid rain or think of it as a bad thing, but rain is really important, and Tiger Rain is no less important for your free-flowing Tiger energy. By condensing and releasing all of your unprocessed emotions, you can move the stress, pain, anger, and frustration through your body and release them back into the ether. If you fail to move the negative energy through you, it can get trapped and fester, making us rigid and dense.

After a good downpour of Tiger Rain, you will feel calm, peaceful, and light. As the droplets leave your body, they make room for you to feel your love and joy once more. It's a beautiful, natural thing. Let it happen.

Feel It All

Sometimes Tigers can expand problems and pain so much that instead of feeling the full range and depths of our emotions and then releasing them through Tiger Rain, we pull back, shut down, and block them out. In essence, we pull away from our powerful Tiger energy and we move toward our Dragon. Instead of feeling *everything*, we strive to feel *nothing*. But pleasure and pain are the two ends of the same feeling continuum, and when Tigers allow themselves to become comfortably numb and indifferent, we block out the pleasure along with the pain. That's what happened to me. I didn't fester, because I didn't feel.

I can't precisely remember the moment when I went numb; it happened sometime in my early twenties when my family's issues were spiraling out of control.

My father is a hardworking, charming, charismatic, and success-ful entrepreneur, as well as a respected leader in our community. He has a big personality, and part of that big personality includes his short fuse and volatile temper. At the drop of a hat, he can switch from laughing and gregarious to antagonistic and hostile. Despite his volatility, he was still the cornerstone of our family all the way up until we had families of our own. His business financially sup-ported the extended family, and we all heavily relied on his strength to guide our daily lives. He was my business mentor, emotional rock, and I really did idolize him. Then just before our wedding, he became clinically, morbidly depressed. During this time, he lost all of his charm and charisma and left behind only the ugly parts of his personality. It took years for him to make a full recovery.

The emotions I embodied during this difficult time were intense. I felt sadness, fear, and anxiety around my father's illness. I missed his charismatic charm and loud, raspy, infectious laugh. I missed his leadership and strength and didn't know if he would be "gone" for-ever. I felt a deep responsibility to support my mother and "save" the family business, and I felt abandoned by our small community who had disassociated from our family during this time of trauma. I felt so much that I subconsciously turned off my feelings. I shied away from my Tiger energy and shifted even deeper into my all-doing Dragon. I put my head down, stopped feeling, and started working.

The following decade I worked harder than I had ever worked and felt the absolute minimal amount needed to survive. I put up emotional walls in every direction and became comfortably numb. I now realize that it was Peter who suffered the most, because I shut him out together with my doubts and pain. I stopped feeling pain, but I also stopped feeling positive emotions and sharing my love and my joy. I was living in a numb emotional wasteland.

Whether it is the loss of a parent or child, sexual abuse, physical abuse, failure, or heartbreak, at some point Tigers can feel so deeply and hurt so much that they choose nothingness. But by living a comfortably numb existence, the Tiger cheats itself out of a full life experience, replete with all the happiness and love that are available in the present moment. It's an absolute tragedy.

There's only one way to feel the depths of your pleasure, and that is by letting go, opening up, and learning to feel it all—pain included. It's time to allow those droplets to condense and then let them go as you allow your Tiger Rain Cloud to rupture.

Embrace the Rupture

It wasn't until the birth of my first daughter, Ophelia, that my droplets started to form. For the first time in over ten years, I felt pure unadulterated joy. I was still holding back, but my emotions were taking form. And during the two years that followed her birth, my condensation commenced; whereas I previously felt a deep lack of passion and desire in my life, I unexpectedly felt desperate to be seen as a sexual being once again. Upon returning to work, I felt frustration and dissatisfaction with my job and the way my business partner was treating me. Looking at my innocent and helpless baby,

I felt, quite unexpectedly, deep hurt and rage toward my father for his volatility. And just as my clouds were getting dark, I saw the photos on Peter's laptop and a new feeling pierced through: betrayal. That final feeling burst me. I ruptured.

It was at that moment that I forgot my walls, forgot my Dragon Training, and felt absolutely everything. My clouds opened and the emotional waters began pouring down. But what I realized was that after I fell apart and felt such immense pain, I was also able to feel immense pleasure and joy again. After I felt betrayed by Peter, I then felt compassion, forgiveness, and—strangely—desire. Peter was seeing me and feeling me again after I was shut off from him for so many years. After I allowed myself to feel rage toward my father for his volatility, I felt a deep respect for him for working as hard as he did and providing the best life for us that he could. I even felt gratitude for my business partner and the training and mentoring he provided.

I needed to allow myself to feel it all. I needed to bathe in the depths of my emotions. Yes, I ruptured, but I survived, I grew, I expanded, and I evolved. Through that process of rupturing, I stopped feeling numb and finally felt not just pain but also pleasure. I finally felt the sunshine on my face.

So now when I am starting to feel a negative emotion, instead of going numb or pulling back, I create the space and time to feel it through. Maybe I skip a workout or cancel a dinner and stay home, put on some sad music, and cry (or play angry rock music and scream). Whatever I need to do to let go and rupture in that moment, I do it.

Now, I no longer try to stifle the emotions of my daughters. When they are angry, we feel it through together. We yell. We read *Grumpy Monkey* and beat our chests like grumpy monkeys. We scream until we laugh. Whatever they need to feel, we practice feeling it together.

Don't be scared to feel your rupture. You won't break apart; you will just break open.

CHAPTER 8

Let Go to Live a Full Tiger Life

If you have ever undertaken a major spring clean or a Marie Kondo–style home overhaul, you always begin the process knowing that your house is going to get a lot messier before it gets cleaner. But you aren't scared of the mess, because on the other side you know the joy that tidiness and organization will bring to your life.

Well, that's exactly where we now are in the pleasure process. Now that you have ruptured, broken open, and started to really "feel it all," things are going to get emotionally messier before you find your way through to your pleasure. You have reached the chaotic second stage of the process, which is the part where you practice *letting go.*

In order to go deep into your Tiger, you will need to learn to let go and live your life with a little less control and a little more abandon. Relinquish your to-do lists and your need to control every decision in every moment. Let go of the guilt surrounding your pleasure, your judgments during sex, and the walls surrounding your heart. Let your life get a little messy. After all, your Tiger energy is your wild, free-flowing, and ethereal energy.

If you're thinking "easier said than done," you're right. We need a simpler place to begin breaking free of the restraints that withhold your wildness. One way to start is by showing us your "Crazy 10."

Show Your "Crazy 10"

Before my rupture, when Peter and I would argue, I would show him about a 3 out of 10 on my "crazy-angry scale." We would yell and fight, as couples do, and I knew I had way more emotion to let out, but I held it back. I would walk away, leave the room, get on a flight, or just "leave it" for another day. And if I didn't walk away, then Peter would. He would see me start to lose it, and he would leave, proving to me that he wasn't really strong enough to handle all of me anyway.

After my rupture, I stopped walking away. I stopped holding back and I started to just let it all go. I finally showed Peter my full *Crazy 10*. Oh, he tried to walk away, but I was able to convince him to sit through it. I knew that if we were going to work through our trauma, he needed to show me his commitment; he needed to show me that he was strong enough to handle my crazy. After all, he was the catalyst for my rupture, the one who had pushed me to my Crazy 10, so the least he could do was sit there and keep me company as I felt it through. To his credit, he did just that: He stood firm and took it all.

To show someone your Crazy 10 and have them stand firm and hold you is a form of soul-quenching pleasure. It's the Tiger's job to let go, and it's the Dragon's job to stand firm and hold it. And now that we have been through my Crazy 10 together, I know beyond a shadow of a doubt that Peter is strong enough to hold me. All of me.

In fact, Peter has learned to love and crave my wildness. He knows that if I am feeling particularly emotional, then I am letting go into my Tiger energy. It doesn't scare him at all, because he knows on the other side he will see my bright light, feel my joy, and witness my pleasure. It's what makes me different from him, and it helps to create Polarity in our relationship.

If you let yourself go and it's too much for your partner, then maybe they aren't the right person for you. You can't temper your emotions out of fear of losing someone, because if you hold back your crazy bad, you're also holding back your crazy good. They are two sides of the same coin, and you and your partner need to learn to embrace both.

I know, I know. It all sounds good in theory, but I can sense your fear. Can you really let go? Show someone your Crazy 10? You absolutely can. In order to make that process a little easier, let's address that deep-seated need you feel for safety.

Leave Your Enclosure

A tiger enclosure at the zoo is perfectly safe: The tiger gets fed and watered each day, it gets regular visits from the veterinarian, and it even gets the opportunity to mate. Life is good. . . . You can see where I'm going with this, can't you?

A life in captivity might be safe, but it isn't wild, and it isn't free. The tiger never gets to feel the pleasure of sprinting at full speed through the savanna, the fear of starvation, or the deep satisfaction that comes from catching and devouring a gazelle. Yes, life is safer in the enclosure, but the enclosure isn't the full life experience.

Prior to discovering Peter's infidelity, I lived my life in an enclosure. I thought I would be safe there. I thought that by withholding my emotions and retreating into my all-doing Dragon energy, I could protect myself from having to feel the sort of pain I felt after my family imploded. But I wasn't any safer living this way, and I certainly wasn't any happier.

It's somewhat of a paradox: The Tiger doesn't want to "let go" until they feel safe, but they won't feel safe until they let go and see that they already are as safe as they possibly can be. The truth is that you can handle life in the wild. You were designed precisely for it.

After my rupture, I had every reason to close my heart again. Peter had lied to me for seventeen years and violated my trust. But I couldn't allow his infidelity to stop me from experiencing my full life; I had already learned that lesson. I had felt my rupture and survived. Now was the time to open up even more.

If you can learn to let go before you feel perfectly safe, that will push you deeper into your Tiger energy, and you will feel power in that abandon. Yes, when you let go and put your heart out there, you might be disappointed, you might get hurt, but it won't break you. You're a ferocious Tiger. You can handle it.

Surrender to the Moment

I can hear you ask, "Okay, I get it, but how do I 'let go'?" A great place to start is to learn to *surrender to the moment.*

Did you have a visceral reaction to those words? A word like "surrender" sounds a lot like "failure," "weakness," and "defeat." That's just an echo of your Dragon training.

Surrendering to the moment requires you to stop trying to control every single moment of your life. Let go and give your mind a rest. Shift the energy that is trapped in your mind and your thoughts and release it down into your heart.

Try it for a few minutes at first, and then work your way up to ten. Intentionally surrender for that time. In those minutes, stop making decisions about your future. Forget your to-do list, your emails. Surrender all expectations and relax in the free flow of the moment. Visualize all of that energy moving from your head down to your heart and opening up your chest. This will probably feel uncomfortable at first, but stick with it.

During the COVID-19 lockdown, I had to learn to really let go. I had spent two years working on a retail business that was now vapor. I had begun writing this book and wanted to keep working on it, but day cares were closed, and I had a two- and three-year-old with a combined attention span of six minutes. No babysitter, nannies, grandparents, or aunts to assist. Peter went into Dragon mode and focused on his business, so I was left with the kids and the house. For the first time in our lives, we had nowhere to go and nowhere we needed to be—no playdates, no dance classes, no swimming lessons, no playgrounds. I had no business to build and no meetings to attend. It was just me, my daughters, our imaginations, and an *entire day* to fill.

After fighting it for a week or two, I finally discovered the pleasure in surrendering to the moment. Getting dressed could now take an hour or even two, since we had nowhere to go. We would slowly fumble with buttons, struggle with socks, change our mind about jackets, reverse the whole process. Taking the dog for a walk would turn into an hour-long hunt for ladybugs. It was beautiful. There was such simple pleasure in the surrender.

When you surrender to the situation at hand, you need to let go of any inner dialogue that might be fighting with that moment. Let go of the plans you made, the things you wanted to accomplish, and embrace the moment that is before you. The more you do it, the more pleasurable you'll find it can feel.

Surrender to the Dragon

You can also learn to "let go" by surrendering your decision-making to your partner.

Now I can really feel your resistance. Would you feel better if I had used the word "delegate"? The problem with delegation is that it implies that you are still responsible for the ultimate decision and outcome, whereas by surrendering you are truly letting go.

So practice surrender. Know that you don't need to make *all* of the decisions *all* of the time. Your Dragon training taught you how to be self-sufficient—you have that badge; you have nothing to prove. Now, in order to embody softness, ease, and that beautiful, carefree Tiger energy, you can't be responsible for making all of the decisions all of the time. Tiger energy is free-flowing, and decisions are a form of structure that will drain you. Where the Dragon becomes strong and energized by making decisions, the Tiger becomes tired and fatigued. So take a break.

Think as if you are a commercial aircraft pilot on a vacation. Yes, you could fly the plane—in fact, you might be the best bloody pilot on the planet—but today, you are on vacation, and your partner is going to fly the plane. Sit back, relax in your first-class seat with your glass of champagne, and let go. I know that is easier said than done when you have 30,000 flying hours under your belt. So just like you practiced flying, you'll need to practice letting go.

Start small. Maybe you relinquish the choice of what to have for dinner, what to watch on TV, or how to spend your Sunday. Starting small will also help your partner with the practice, too, because they will initially think it is a trick or a test. If you surrender your movie selection, they may think you are really saying, "Do you love me enough to remember what movie I said I wanted to see last week?" You'll have to reassure them that it is not a test and show them that you won't judge the process or the outcome; you just want to be a passenger for this moment.

Instead of making decisions, make it your goal to give love and joy to the moment. Where you would usually think about what you are doing, observe and feel instead. Feel the good and the bad—if your Dragon is floundering and you hate their crappy sci-fi movie choice, release your judgment and laugh at how insignificant the decision was in the first place. Snuggle in and enjoy the popcorn.

I have surrendered all of the decisions for our Saturday date night to Peter. I let him choose the restaurant, organize the sitter, and get the kids dinner. I even let him hold the door for me (something I never used to let him do). After dinner, I let him ravish me and surrender to his lovemaking. But this beautiful date night experience didn't happen overnight; it took practice. I had to learn to surrender—not only the decisions themselves, but also my judgment of Peter's decisions. It took a while for Peter to get used to it, too, and to trust that I would really let go and not swoop in at the last minute and take over. Yet after persevering and experiencing the power of the practice, it's now the highlight of our week. Peter takes it seriously and spends time and energy thinking about how to impress me, and I am deeply relieved to have an evening off from planning. All I do now is take the time and space to make myself feel and look beautiful, and I walk out our front door at 6 p.m.

If you're not yet in a long-term relationship, you can test this practice of surrender on a date. Practice being a passenger. Truly let go. Surrender every decision, and see how you feel. Do it intentionally and with presence, but relax and have fun with the process. I promise you that you'll notice a change in the energy on your date. If you must, explain what you are doing to your date: Tell them that you want to surrender into your pleasure, and that requires you to surrender your decision-making. The more fun and playful you can make it, the more they will buy into the process. You'll be amazed by how much fun you can both have when you let go.

CHAPTER 9

Feel the Pleasure

You've come a long way. You've broken open and survived your rupture. You've surrendered to the moment and to the Dragon and let it all go. Now the fun part: You get to feel all the way through to your pleasure.

Feeling your pleasure will help release you and relax you into your ethereal Tiger energy. A Tiger who learns to fully embody their pleasure will shine a light so bright it will inspire everyone in their path. That's the power of the pleasure-filled Tiger.

Accessing that pleasure is not an intellectual phenomenon. It doesn't happen in your thinking—you have to feel it in your body. It is also not something anyone can give you. You can't rely on anyone else for your feeling of pleasure; only you can feel it for yourself.

It's your pleasure, and it's time to prioritize it.

Prioritize Yourself

Easier said than done. Tigers are notorious for putting the needs of their family and friends ahead of their own pleasure. The reason is that many Tigers believe that sacrifice and deprivation are how you show people you love them. And while it can be gratifying when such self-sacrifice is acknowledged and appreciated, most of the time it will barely be noticed—which means that most prolonged periods of self-deprivation only end with feelings of resentment and sadness.

But why does it need to be an either/or scenario? You can experience love and joy through caring and nurturing for those you love while also prioritizing your own pleasure. It all comes down to how you frame it.

First, you need to know what actually brings you joy. Can you answer that question? You'll need to be honest with yourself here. I ultimately had to ignore my Dragon Training to finally admit that I found pleasure in cooking dinner for my family. Don't get me wrong, some days it is an absolute grind (particularly when a little picky eater refuses to taste my meal), but there is something I find extremely pleasurable about making a delicious, nourishing meal for my family. Yet to find the pleasure in the act of cooking dinner, I had to let go of my outdated feminist ideals that I "would never slave away in the kitchen for a man." My old brain training was getting in the way of my pleasure.

Be honest: If nurturing others brings you pleasure, feel that pleasure. If it doesn't, then do what you can to get it done as quickly as possible (or outsource it to someone else if you can) so you can move on and make room for the things that *do* bring you pleasure.

While they may not want to admit it, many Tigers subconsciously prioritize the pleasure of others because it is often easier than feeling their own pleasure. Prioritizing pleasure is not something our purpose-driven society teaches Tigers to do, so we don't really know where to start. If you were to ask a Tiger, "What will make you happy?" most will struggle to give an honest and accurate answer. Tigers will likely approach the problem before them in the manner in which they approach all problems: They will make it bigger.

A Tiger may think, "I'll be happy when I'm seen and loved for my beautiful, perfectly finished home, my curated and cleaned-out closet, my ability to play an instrument, my fluent French . . ." Tigers put up obstacles to their pleasure to the point that they make it unattainable for themselves, which in turn makes focusing on and delivering other people's pleasure easier. Tigers can then blame those around them for their unhappiness and hide behind the demands of their partner, family, job, and friends. But believe you me, other people don't want that. They don't want to be the reason you are unhappy.

How many times have you heard your partner say, "I just want you to be happy"? It can be hard to trust that sentiment, but your Dragon really does want to see you happy and filled with pleasure. Everyone does, but no one more than your Dragon. The Dragon wants to see you smile, shine, dance, laugh, and even scream with delight—*that's* the energy that the Dragon craves.

Start to find the things in life that bring you pleasure and work on including them every day. They don't need to be huge. If you're having trouble coming up with things that seem feasible, try journaling a list of what brings you joy. *Feel* into this activity; don't think about it. *Feel* your heart swelling with joy as you write down something that deeply pleases you. You will likely be surprised at how short, modest, and attainable your true pleasures are. A perfectly flavored scoop of ice cream, a smooch with the dog, a meaningful conversation with a friend, a good night's sleep, or even a good cup of coffee can all work. Okay, so maybe you also have Burning Man or the soccer World Cup on your list, but for the most part, it will be life's beautiful moments that give you pleasure. The only thing between you and your pleasure is your prioritization of it, your state of mind, and your acknowledgment of the moments. Finding our pleasure isn't nearly as complicated as we make it out to be.

Attach an Obligation to the Pleasure

If, after recognizing what brings you pleasure, prioritizing those things is too hard for you to do, then a good solution is to attach obligation. I know that sounds strange, but sometimes we need a kick in the pants to do what's right for us.

While it is very difficult for Tigers to say yes to their own pleasure, it is very easy for them to say yes to responsibility and obligation. *That* they know how to do. Tigers are highly motivated when they can be of service to someone else.

Perhaps you love live concerts. Book tickets for you and a friend, put it in the calendar, and know that they are looking forward to the evening as much as you are. By doing this, the chances of you blowing off or otherwise missing the event get dramatically reduced.

For me, I feel a deep obligation to my personal trainer. I have been training with Cassi for five years, and I know if I don't turn up, it messes with her day and her calendar. I also know she runs a small business, so she relies on me as a client to live her life. This sense of obligation gets my ass to the studio three times a week, even when I'm tired, hungover, or feeling gross. Whatever I am feeling, I feel it with her in the studio, and I always leave infinitely happier.

Fill Up

Because Tigers are notorious for subconsciously operating with a "self-sacrifice" mindset, they will actually ignore and miss many moments in their lives that have the potential to fill them up with pleasure.

I used to constantly complain that I didn't have enough time in my day to write because I have to take the girls to their after-school activities, namely dance class. So Peter, being the Dragon he is, tried to solve my problem: He offered to get a nanny to pick up the kids after school and take them where they needed to go. I immediately protested that it was an unnecessary house-hold expense (another self-sacrifice), but when I was honest with myself, I recognized that watching those toddlers in their pink tutus was one of the most pleasurable moments of my week. So instead of feeding the rhetoric of self-sacrifice, I now acknowl-edge that I want to take my daughters to their dance classes, and I make sure I find pleasure in that hour. (As it turns out, I have plenty of time to write when I organize my days better.)

To really experience the joy of watching my daughters dance, I take a second to acknowledge the moment and visualize my plea-sure as a bright white light filling up my heart with love. I breathe into it and feel my heart expand until it nearly bursts out of my chest. Once I have found a moment of pleasure and filled up as much as I can, I try to feel into it by sharing my pleasure with oth-ers who will appreciate it. In this example, I'll often FaceTime my mom to share about the dance class. Whatever it is, I try to brag about it, laugh about it, talk about it, share it, and make the pleasure last longer by dragging it out and building it up.

Your days are full of moments and people that have the ability to provide you with soul-quenching pleasure. It's your job to iden-tify those moments, lean in, and savor every last drop of your joy. It's your pleasure. Indulge in it.

Indulge Your Sensations

If you're having trouble identifying those moments, events, and people that give you pleasure, then start even smaller and try to focus on your sensations. Every inch of your body was anatomically designed to help you find pleasure, so reconnect with your body and indulge your senses.

Orgasms aside, one of the fastest ways to attain pleasure is via our sense of touch. I was amazed to learn that each fingertip has more than 3,000 touch receptors, many of which respond primarily to pressure. Our tongues and lips are equally as sensitive. So it's no surprise that kissing, eating, drinking, massage, and holding hands are quick ways for Tigers to attain pleasure.

Tigers also love to indulge in pleasure through their sense of smell. It's no accident that the fragrance industry generates over $90 billion annually.[1] Most Dragons are confused by the Tiger's obsession with candles and perfume, which allow a Tiger to take a moment for sensorial indulgence. Similarly, the smell of a cigar, the ocean air, a warm fire, a freshly mown lawn, or a flower from a childhood garden all take a Tiger deep into their pleasure centers and fill them with love. Next time you're eating a perfect meal or smelling freshly ground coffee, take a moment, open your heart, and visualize your physical body filling up with a bright white light of pleasure.

Finding your pleasure takes practice, and that takes time. When I started to indulge my senses and lean into my pleasure, I got better at finding my joy and happiness on my own. I would go for a walk on the beach, take a warm bath, or smell some fresh flowers, and I would feel my deep pleasure. But within an hour of the kids and Peter arriving, poof! It was vapor. I found it really hard to keep that radiance flowing when my peace intersected with my chaotic life, but I kept listening to my body and seeking out my pleasure, and slowly that inner light started to shine through in my day-to-day.

---

1 According to Statista from 2018 data, https://www.statista.com/topics/1008/cosmetics-industry/#dossierKeyfigures.

It rose closer to the surface and became easier to access. It was just a spark at first—a more enjoyable dinner with the family or a fun community sing-along to "Let It Go." I am not aiming for full-time pleasure: merely a sprinkle throughout the day. The more you indulge in your pleasure, the easier it will become.

Tiger Time

Filling an open Tiger heart with enough pleasure and love is like filling a sandcastle moat with water at the beach—it's a constant and endless work in progress. And while you can certainly do it alone, that's a lot of work, and it can be a little lonely. It's okay to recruit help. After all, Tiger energy grows strong through connection.

When you're looking for help filling up with pleasure, the Dragons in your life can certainly lend a hand, but keep in mind that Dragons aren't energized by the same things you are. Don't be surprised if your Dragon runs out of puff long before your open heart is full.

In the same way that Dragon energy grows strong by spending time with other Dragons, Tiger energy is expanded by spending time *feeling* with other Tigers. So consciously spend time with your Tiger friends, your Tiger family members (at least the ones you get along with), your Tiger children, your Tiger community—whoever it is, wherever it is, find those Tigers who bring you pleasure, and prioritize your time with them. If your Dragon partner protests your time away, explain what you are doing, and they will likely be happy that you are prioritizing your pleasure. (Remember, they just want you to be happy.)

It isn't always easy to find Tiger time, and every Tiger feels pleasure differently, but don't let that be an excuse. I live in Florida, but my best Tiger friends live in England and Australia. My London-based bestie has some anxiety/control issues that stop her from answering the phone, so we have to connect via text, email, or WhatsApp. Instead of controlling her quirks, I have learned to embrace and love them. Some mornings I will wake up to seventy-two WhatsApp messages and will laugh out loud at her wildness as she writes from topic to topic in an untethered stream of consciousness. Another Tiger friend in Australia has two toddler boys, so she barely has a moment free, let alone a spare hand to write a text. We connect via voice recordings. On our daily walks, we record long-winded, unfiltered voice messages and send them off to each other. We each listen when we have a spare moment with no pressure to respond. Each one is a strand of connection that pulls us closer and fills our hearts with love. Then, of course, there's my mom, who insists we always use FaceTime video (even if she is in a crowded, noisy restaurant). She doesn't care if my hair is a mess, my house is a mess, my life is a mess—she wants to see my face and share in my life.

In the end, when you let go, open your heart, and fill it with pleasure and love, your light will shine so bright that people will be drawn to you like a beacon in the night.

How to Feel the Tiger

Learning to let go and feel into my Tiger was by far the hardest thing I have had to do in my life. I had no experience, no training, and no idea of how my life would look outside my enclosure. I spent a lifetime convincing myself that I was safe and comfortable in my numbness, but, as I abruptly discovered, I had been no safer in my enclosure than I was living freely in the wild. I not only survived my rupture and my Tiger Rain, but I also thrived because it broke my heart open. The wider I opened my heart, the more pleasure I was free to feel, and the happier I became.

I now feel deeply seen and loved, not just in my relationship, but in every area of my life as well. I am free to feel my pleasure and let go into my wildness. If I can do it, I know you can, too.

Living a Full Tiger Life

Here's a summary of the steps you can take to leave your enclosure, open your heart, and find your own bliss:

1. Stop chasing external validation. Any pleasure you feel from being intensely seen and loved by an external source will be fleeting and shallow. Find your real love by *feeling* the infinite love that's available to you in the present moment.

2. Feel more pleasure by opening your heart and feeling *everything*. Pleasure and pain are the two ends of the same continuum, so you need to let go to feel it all— even the pain—to tap into that pleasure.

3. Stop waiting to feel safe. You are already safe. You won't break—you will just break open.

4. Show your partner your Crazy 10. They can handle it (or they can't, and maybe you need a new partner).

5. Surrender. Surrender to the moment. Surrender your decision-making. Surrender to your Dragon. Feel the natural, untethered wildness within you when you let go.

6. Stop overcomplicating your pleasure. Start small, find the pleasure in life's micro-moments, and lean into what you find.

7. Push deep into your Tiger energy by continually prioritizing your pleasure, indulging your senses, and filling up through connection (particularly with other Tigers).

PART IV

Creating Polarity

The sad reality of relationships today is that most of us are coasting through life in a dull numbness of coexistence. We are spending so much uninterrupted time with our partner that it has created a crisis of energetic and sexual neutrality. Like magnets, we have rubbed up against each other for so long and with such consistency that we have completely dulled the powerful attraction we once had. In order to get it back, we need to intentionally create space. That is what this chapter is all about.

By now you should have a pretty good feeling for which energy you more naturally embody. You should also have a fairly good idea of which energy your partner possesses.

Here's a quick (albeit overly simplified) energy summary:

DRAGON	TIGER
Controlled, focused	Free, open, radiant
Grounded, purpose-driven	Wild, emotion-driven
Seeks challenge	Seeks love and nurture
Single-task oriented	Multitask oriented
Wants freedom and release	Wants to gather and fill up
Makes big things small	Makes small things big
Forgets	Remembers
Needs admiration and appreciation	Needs reassurance and attention
Wants to be needed and respected	Wants safety and connection

Seeing our contrasting energy traits listed out like this may make it appear as though our energy is binary when it is anything but. Our energy is fluid; it's moving all the time, and we are all complex beings! For the purposes of this chapter, however, I am intentionally oversimplifying our very complex and fluid energy, because to create Polarity we need someone in the relationship to be a Dragon and someone to be a Tiger, even if for a few hours or a few days. Only then can you create space and create Polarity.

The good news is that most couples are naturally opposed. The bad news is that we tend to get so caught up in our busy, energy-neutral lives that we don't always get a chance to feel the space between us. During the pre-kids decade when Peter and I coexisted in our dual-Dragon life, we would experience glimpses of our potential Polarity from time to time, in particular while we were on vacations. I remember on one particular ten-day vacation to Barbados, Peter spent his days reading business books, becoming inspired and motivated with direction and purpose (grounding into his Dragon), while I totally "switched off" and read the romance series *Fifty Shades of Grey* (relaxing into my Tiger). Within a day or two of reading, drinking, and lying by the pool, we finally felt our conflict melt away. We were drawn to each other once again; we started to make love, talk, and intimately connect. At the end of the vacation we looked at each other and hoped we could stay in this moment, this energy, forever. Peter turned to me, looked me in the eyes with a little sadness, and said, "I've missed you. I've missed this."

Then, we returned to our dual-Dragon lives and disconnected once again.

Of course, it's easy to sigh and say, "My partner will never change. They're too set in their ways." We are all conditioned by small, routine experiences with our partner to believe that "this is how they are." But have you ever seen your partner in a different environment (like on vacation) or around different people (like their work friends) and thought, "Wow, you are a completely different person"? Yes, they are! Our experience of our partner is only *our* energetic experience. When we inject different energy into our relationship, we all have the ability to behave radically differently, just like Peter and I occasionally experienced on our vacations. And it's those unknown outcomes that make this process of generating Polarity sexy and exciting.

Fortunately, you don't need to wait for a vacation to find Polarity. You can learn how to encourage your partner to go deeper into their Dominant Energy each day. It's a skill that will serve you well in creating and maintaining that "happy place" where there is more flow, pleasure, and desire in your life.

The tools in the following chapters are designed to help you push your partner deeper into their dominance, with or without their participation, so you can experience that "vacation feeling" every day. The first chapter shows Dragons what they can do to help their Tiger partner dive deeper into their Tiger energy; the following chapter does the opposite, showing Tigers how to push their Dragon partner deeper into their Dragon energy. If, after deep consideration, you believe you and your partner are energetically the same (e.g., Tiger/Tiger or Dragon/Dragon) and you want sexual Polarity from the relationship, you will need to learn to temporarily push or pull into an opposing pole. We'll cover that in more detail in the final chapter.

CHAPTER 10

Dragons: Love Your Tigers

During one winter break, Peter and I spent an afternoon playing soccer on the beach with the kids, jumping off sand dunes and being generally very silly. When we got home, Peter grabbed my hands, looked me in the eyes, and said, "I love seeing you playing and having fun with the girls. It's hard for me to describe how it makes me feel, but you look so beautiful and sexy, and it just makes me want to make love to you. It *really* makes me want to have another baby with you. It makes me so happy to see you like that."

Wow. Peter fucking nailed it.

I felt so seen and loved by those words, particularly because he physically grabbed me, held my hands, and gazed into my eyes when he said them. He was fully conscious. While having another baby is definitely not my desired outcome, he deeply rewarded me for feeling my pleasure, and that made me want to continue feeling it. It was the ultimate reward for my fun—the encouragement to have *more fun.*

That's what it takes for a Dragon to both support and set free their Tiger partner.

So let me speak to all the Dragons out there: In the same way you believe you will be happy when you are free, your Tiger partner believes they will be happy when they have received enough love. And the true love that nourishes them and brings them happiness comes from holding love in their heart and pleasure in their body. (If this sounds a bit woo-woo, it means you probably skipped reading Part III. Go back there and learn what makes your Tiger partner tick!)

Despite popular belief (and likely your own self-confidence), there is nothing *you* can *do* to make your Tiger feel happy. Maybe I need to repeat that: There's nothing you can do to make your partner feel happy. Your Tiger must find a way to feel their own happiness. That being said, if you want to see your partner go deeper into that free, wild, pleasure-filled Tiger energy that you so deeply crave, you will need to stop sitting back and waiting and hoping, because there's a lot you can do to bring out that pleasure-filled Tiger in your partner—and reward them when it happens.

It all starts by creating a safe space so your Tiger can *let go*.

Create a Safe Space for Tigers

Before your partner will fully embody their Tiger, they must feel safe to do so. This means knowing you are there to watch their back (and their world) while they relax.

Imagine going to the pool to relax, but when you lie down on your towel, you notice, out of the corner of your eye, an unaccompanied toddler without floaties just splashing around in the pool. No parent in sight. Can you really drink your cocktail and take a nap with the toddler in your periphery? Of course not. Well, that's how the Tiger feels about *everything*.

Your Tiger has invested countless hours, days, and years building a beautiful, safe, loving home and life for themselves. They need to know that after they are done having fun, there will still be a home to come back to, not a pile of rubble. That confidence comes from consistent assurances—and demonstrations—that you've "got this."

The sense of safety that Tiger energy needs in order to come out and play comes from many micro-moments, not just the big ones. It's not enough that you make the mortgage payment on time each month, get the car serviced before a vacation, stock up on Costco supplies before a hurricane, or that you fastidiously keep your credit score at 850. While those things help a Tiger to feel safe, you need to do the small things, too, if you want to help your Tiger relax each day.

Some days I will call Peter and ask him to pick something up on his way home, like a loaf of bread or a prescription refill. He used to say yes no matter what, but that didn't mean that he would actually pick it up. Peter believed that saying yes would make me happy (and he really does want to make me happy). If he remembered and actually picked up the bread, it made my day slightly easier. But if he said he would pick it up and then forgot, that made my day harder. Picking up the bread won't make me happy, but forgetting to pick up the bread after saying he would *will* make me very unhappy. This small failure to follow through erodes trust. It makes me feel as if his word isn't solid and that I can't depend on him to follow through on his promises. This tiny act of saying one thing and doing another pushes me deep into my Dragon energy. It reminds me that I can't rely on anyone but myself.

Every time you don't follow through on a promise, no matter how small, the Tiger thinks, "I'll just do it for myself," which moves them deeper into their Dragon energy. Of course the Tiger can do it for themselves. They've had a lifetime of training to be self-sufficient, same as you. Yet even though a Tiger *can* do it all, deep down (and this is hard for them to admit), they really don't want to. They want the same thing you want for them: to throw their hands up in the air and have some fun. Yet to do that requires a great deal of vulnerability—which is why it's your role to make them feel safe.

Peter now understands this, and instead of saying yes to everything in order to appease me, he stands firmly behind his "no" when he says it. When he says no, I thank him for his honesty and then I either go without the bread, prescription, or so forth, or I get it myself. Because he set a boundary, I respect him for that. That is integrity I can trust. That makes me feel safe.

Ultimately, life's micro-moments become a series of tiny Tiger tests designed by the Tiger (usually subconsciously) to determine whether they can let go and find their pleasure. Will you continue to hold their world together when they release the reins? When you pick up the bread, take out the trash, pay the speeding ticket—essentially when you follow through on your word, you are demonstrating your strong, reliable Dragon core. When you don't follow through, your Tiger sees your Dragon core as weak, and they cannot trust you to keep them safe. Consistent clarity, direction, integrity, and presence will all make your Tiger feel safe.

When your Tiger feels safe, they will then be more receptive to letting you lead them to a place where they can let go and feel into their deep Tiger pleasure. This brings me to the second lesson: learning to lead your Tiger to their pleasure.

Take the Lead

If a Tiger can do everything you can do (and possibly better), then why do they need you? What is your value? Ultimately, the value of the Dragon for the Tiger is to lead them to places that they cannot take themselves. If you can help lead your partner from their mind into their body, from their "doing" into their "feeling," and from their Dragon into their Tiger with your presence and depth of consciousness, your Tiger will shower you with light and devotion. That is a promise.

The reality is that unless your Tiger partner is working in an industry that allows them to embody love, fluidity, and creativity at work, they are likely spending most of their day in their Dragon energy. If they are a homemaker, they are definitely spending their day in the Dragon "doing" mode. As the dominant Dragon, you can help your Tiger shed their Dragon skin and move into their Tiger energy when they finish their workday. This can be a little harder if your partner is a homemaker or working from home, because there aren't clear "workday" boundaries, but as a Dragon, you need to help create boundaries so that they have the space and time to let go.

It took a real effort for both Peter and me to embody this practice. Peter would usually walk into our house after work and download granular details of his progress and challenges that day. We would analyze them together, and I would help him with any business guidance or insights I could provide. But that wasn't fulfilling for me, and, after a long day of work (and later homemaking), it really felt like more work. Plus he didn't actually need my guidance; it was just an old habit we had formed. So we made a conscious effort to break this habit. Initially he missed the daily debrief, but now he calls a fellow Dragon on his drive home and has that conversation with them instead. Then, when he walks through the door at home, he throws on some music, pours a glass of wine, and focuses on sharing the positive headlines and fun anecdotes that happened during his day. I enjoy our post-work conversations so much more now, and the music and frivolity help me shed my Dragon skin instead of trapping myself in it.

Still, shedding my Dragon skin is harder on some days than on others. When I get deep into my Dragon "doing" mode, it's hard to break the momentum! So sometimes in order to lead your Tiger deeper into their energy, you may need to intervene physically. Try giving them a big, strong, comforting hug and then gaze deeply into their eyes. Don't give up if they don't respond at first; in fact, they will likely try to look over your shoulder or pull away. Be strong. Be the fucking Dragon and keep gazing. Keep looking until you can see their heart and they can see your resolve.

If that is just too extreme for you (or for them), try turning on some music and encouraging them to dance or to sit for ten minutes and relax while you give them a shoulder rub, make them a cup of tea, or pour them a glass of wine. If they are in Dragon mode, I assure you, they will fight you on this. When a Tiger is in their Dragon mode, they have lots of "things to do" and places to be; they don't have time for shoulder rubs and dancing! Your partner will say, "I have to cook dinner," or "I have emails to send," but no matter what they say, persevere and lead. Acknowledge what needs to be done, and then instruct them that as soon as they have sent those emails or cooked dinner, it's time to stop and relax. Run them a bath and then lead them there when they have finished whatever task they "had to do." Deliver them to a place they won't deliver themselves, a place where they can let go and find pleasure.

In order to lead your Tiger to their pleasure, you are going to have to pay attention. You will know what brings them pleasure when you see it because they will light up from within and appear energized and free—so start making mental notes. Does your Tiger look relaxed and happy after a run, meditation, a bath, singing along with a song, or walking with the dog? Watch for those little things that help your Tiger relax into their happy place.

Once you know what brings your Tiger into their pleasure, lead them to those things more often. Deep Tiger energy lives in a state of play where the Tiger wants to feel safe, surrender, and be led to their pleasure, only to escape to do the dance all over again. So you need to find a way to start the dance.

Tigers are a sucker for obligation, so if need be, attach an obligation to the pleasure. Buy the tickets. Prepay for dinner. Lock down that pleasure in advance. Let your Tiger know it's not just an idea—it's a done deal. Don't say, "Maybe we should drop your kids with my parents this weekend and get away." Book the hotel, call your folks, and make it happen.

Sometimes the Tiger will also need you to lead them to a place where they will find sexual pleasure. There are occasions when I will get so caught up in my head that the idea of reaching an orgasm just doesn't seem possible. We'll be having sex, and I'll still be thinking about a thousand things from the day. I'm trapped in my mind and not connected with my body. On these occasions I'll say things like, "Don't worry about me; I won't get there tonight," but Peter has learned to try and lead me there anyway. He will say, "Of course you can, just relax. I have nowhere to be, and I can keep doing this all night if I need to." With those simple words, he leads me to a place where I can let go. He makes me feel seen and loved, and he leads me back into my body. Within minutes of his reassurance, I always find my pleasure.

When you do finally see your Tiger light up, be sure to reward that pleasure with your full attention and consciousness. Make sure they know how much you love it when they shine. In other words (and as we'll describe in our next lesson), learn to reward feelings.

Reward Feelings

Every time you encourage your partner's rational, logical, purpose- and mission-based initiatives, and every time you criticize their wildness and emotions, you are drawing your partner away from their Tiger and into their Dragon. This is what you do because this is what you know. It is easy, drama-free, and the path of least resistance.

And despite being drained by it, your Tiger will embody that Dragon energy because that is how they get your attention, and ultimately they want to please you and be seen and loved by you. When your Tiger partner is grounded and motivated, that makes you proud. You respect it, it builds trust (for you), and all of that forms a solid friendship. But it *will not* inspire you (or them) sexually.

Instead, find a way of rewarding your Tiger for finding their feelings. When you see your Tiger in their Tiger energy, encourage them with your words, your love, and most importantly with your attention and consciousness.

Now here's the hard part: It's not just pleasure that you need to reward, but all feelings. I know, that sounds a little scary, but the four-lettered "F" word *feel* is the most powerful tool in your Dragon toolbox. And before you ask, no, you are not going to have to constantly talk about *your* feelings; however, in order for your Tiger to go deeper into their Tiger energy, you need to reward them when *they* start to feel or share their feelings. Because when a Tiger is feeling, they are out of their head and into their hearts, and that is where a Tiger grows strong in their energy.

When your Tiger comes home and starts venting about a problem at work, instead of solving it, ask how that makes them *feel*. Or when your Tiger starts complaining about their family (again), don't try to fix it: Merely ask how that makes them feel. Be sure to listen consciously to their response.

This is particularly important when you believe your Tiger partner has set an irrational boundary or is upset by something that seems illogical to you—please don't try to analyze it. Instead, stay grounded in your Dragon consciousness and try to find out how they are feeling.

For example, I have an irrational boundary when it comes to housework, and that boundary is taking out the trash. I will do absolutely everything around the house, I'll even plunge the toilet when it needs it, but when it comes to taking out the trash, I simply refuse. When Peter finally asked me why, I launched into a long tirade about how he should do more around the house, how unappreciated I was, and how that all made me feel like his full-time housekeeper. And as I wound myself up, he went deeper and asked me, "When you take out the trash, how does that make you *feel?*" That stopped me dead in my tracks. I had to stop ranting and start feeling. I had to listen to my heart.

What I realized when I listened to my feelings was that the trash bag was just symbolic of all of the work that I do that remains unseen. The trash is the output of the hard work that I want him to see and acknowledge. *Look at all these things in the trash bag, that is what I did today. See it, see me, appreciate me, love me."* When I take out the trash, the house feels too perfect, like a hotel. It looks as if it was easy, and I feel as if I am a hotel staff member, untipped and taken for granted.

The funny thing is that after Peter understood how taking out the trash made me feel, he stopped waiting for me to leave it at the door. Now, as the trash gets close to full, he takes it out. At that time, he also stops and thanks me for all the things I do that I think go unseen and unappreciated—he even lists them. I had no idea he'd ever noticed. Peter, the Dragon Master, nailing it once again.

Claim the "Dragon Throne"

The final way you can help your partner ease into their Tiger energy is by taking the "Dragon Throne." When you take the Dragon Throne, you are in a state of deep consciousness. You are calm and grounded. You are the vessel of strength ready to hold the Tiger energy.

You can use the Dragon Throne to evoke the Tiger energy from your partner. To do this, you need to take the throne and then stay there; don't move. It might take fifteen minutes, it might take two days, but continue to claim the throne, and watch as your partner relaxes into their Tiger.

Peter does this effectively by making himself a cup of coffee and sitting alone in silence on the patio while staring out at the ocean. I won't notice him at first because I am busy "doing stuff," but after about fifteen minutes of mentally clocking where he is and what he is doing, I'll find myself stopping my tasks midway and going to join him. I am so drawn to his stillness—I want to be around it. It relaxes my nervous system and helps me to feel into my body and my heart.

To take the throne, try meditating for ten minutes, taking twenty deep breaths into your stomach, or practicing being very still and quiet in your mind and body. You can also use the guided meditation from Part II. (See Page 60.) All of these activities will ultimately sit you in your Dragon Throne. Then take that depth and stillness, go to where your partner is, and continue to be still. Whether it takes five minutes or an hour, I assure you, if you remain deep, still, and conscious, at some point your partner will notice and be drawn to you. Watch them soften and open to you. When they do, reward them with your love and attention.

CHAPTER 11

Tigers: Respect Your Dragons

Now that we have loaded up the Dragons with plenty of homework, it's time to talk to my Tigers.

Hello, Tigers.

Are you ready to nudge your Dragons further into the depths of their power? Because there's a lot you can do to encourage that deep, sexy Dragon stability that you crave.

Firstly, as we covered in Part II, remember that your Dragon is motivated by a deep and unquenchable thirst for freedom. Your Dragon believes that they will be happy when they are free, and that freedom might be physical, financial, or even sexual in nature (plus it can change from day to day). Yet the true, soul-quenching freedom that they deeply desire is freedom from their own self-judgment and ego. And while a Dragon must find that freedom for themselves, there are things you can do to help them on their journey—and make them even more deeply desirable to you.

The most effective method to help your Dragon partner push deeper into their energy is through positive reinforcement. By supporting their purpose, surrendering to their decisions, rewarding their presence, and respecting their achievements, you can help your Dragon find their freedom. Your Dragon will then worship and desire you in return—that is a promise.

Support the Dragon's Purpose

The Dragon's desire for freedom is at the heart of everything they do, including choosing their partner. It is likely that your Dragon was deeply attracted to you and ultimately "chose" you because you supported their quest for personal freedom—whatever that meant to them at that time (financial freedom, spiritual freedom, sexual freedom, etc.).

Over time your Dragon partner may have evolved beyond that initial quest for freedom. They may now be on a new mission, or perhaps they are lost and aimless, without purpose. Since you're the intuitive Tiger partner, understanding where your Dragon is on their journey and supporting them to fulfil their current purpose (or find one) is incredibly powerful in a relationship.

If your Dragon partner has a current purpose or mission, encouraging them to work on it and rewarding them for doing so will help drive them deeper into their Dragon energy. They might be striving to earn a promotion, save the dolphins, learn to road bike, play chess, or arrange flowers; whatever it is, encourage that sense of purpose and help to create the time and space they need to pursue it. That might mean taking on additional responsibilities to give them more time to work on their purpose, or it might mean biting your tongue if you don't think their purpose is meaningful. In fact, criticizing their purpose will undermine the whole operation—it will make them resent you and will do nothing to foster their Dragon energy. You are better off supporting their purpose, even if you don't love it, so that your Dragon can achieve it as quickly as possible and grow into a new one.

On the flip side, if your partner is between purposes, they may seem a little lost. They may not even know they are "purposeless," but as an intuitive Tiger, you can see it. A purposeless Dragon looks like a rudderless boat, floating along and filling their days with toxic nothingness like watching excessive TV, eating, drinking, or playing video games. These are all signs that your Dragon is lost and searching for freedom in all the wrong places. There's nothing less sexy to a Tiger than a Dragon without purpose.

Sometimes an external event will occur that will even drag your usually determined Dragon into the ether of their Tiger energy. If you're paying attention you'll know when it happens: They may seem a little more sensitive, attentive, and insecure, or they may suddenly appear directionless and deflated. In all likelihood, if you are in your Tiger energy at that time, you will feel physically repulsed by them. (If you happen to be in your Dragon energy and you find yourself attracted to this version of your partner, hell, just roll with it and have some fun.)

During one recent Christmas season, Peter had an important client leave his business. He had been advising her for several years and was very attached to the account, as she provided important monthly income that helped him manage his cash flow. It was a painful blow. I knew he had been knocked out of his Dragon energy and into his Tiger because all he wanted to do was talk about the problem with me, with his friends, with his partners, with his parents . . . with the cat. . . . He talked and talked and talked about this problem for almost three weeks. It was exhausting to witness, particularly because he wasn't solving anything—he was just talking. He spent so long in his Tiger energy during those weeks that I became physically repulsed by him. I just couldn't listen anymore! I wanted him to solve the bloody problem and move forward. His Tiger energy was slowly but surely pushing me into my Dragon, where I get uncomfortable and drained if I spend too long in it. I needed to give him a nudge back into his Dragon and fast!

By losing a major client, Peter momentarily felt as if he'd failed at his purpose and "lost the competition." He started to say things like "I don't even know what I'm doing with my life" and "I don't know why I bother. Maybe I should start again and do something new." Even though my inner Dragon wanted to reason with him, this was not the time because he was feeling and not reasoning. Instead I tried to engage his Dragon by giving him a purpose.

I decided to buy skateboards for everyone for Christmas. Peter is a great skater, so by skating around the neighborhood he got out of his head and back into his body. The activity is all about balance and concentration, and it forced him to connect his mind and body in order to skate well. Along with the skateboard, I also gave him a clear purpose: to teach the family how to skate. This meant that he had to lead us and coach us through this life lesson. For starters, he needed to face his fear as a father that the girls would get hurt (fear can be great Dragon fuel). On top of that, I am an absolutely terrible skater. I once broke my wrist falling off a skateboard and am petrified that I will do it again. So by allowing Peter to take me out and teach me, I was showing him that I trusted him and respected him with a very fragile part of myself. I trusted that he wouldn't let me get hurt.

In sum, I re-energized Peter's Dragon not only by giving him a purpose, but also by encouraging physical energy embodiment (the act of skating), presence (through his concentration on skating and teaching), leadership (letting him teach us), respect (from me and the kids), and trust (that he wouldn't let us get hurt). It didn't matter that the new purpose was unrelated to the loss of a client in his business. The skateboard adventure gave Peter a clear focus.

By the end of the afternoon, my Peter-Dragon was back. He stopped talking about his problems and started solving for the year ahead. By the end of the weekend he was ready to get back to his business and I was ready to sleep with him. Everyone was happy.

You can put this example into practice by encouraging your Dragon to participate in activities that demand their presence and concentration. Anything that will help reconnect their mind with their body will work, from hiking or yoga to meditation, painting, building, surfing, or golf. These activities foster purpose and competition. They give a Dragon a sense of space and freedom, and it pushes them back into their consciousness through breath and focus.

All of which brings me to the next lesson: decision-making. Because once your Dragon has zeroed in on a purpose, you can start to encourage them to make more decisions that are aligned behind that purpose. This will help to push them even deeper into their power.

Encourage a Dragon's Decision-making

Dragons grow deep and strong in their energy by making decisions that are aligned behind their mission and purpose. But really, making any decision will help a Dragon go deeper into their power. Decision-making is a form of freedom, and even if the decision is something small, like what music to listen to or where to eat, it will count as a freedom to your Dragon.

That being said, it can be really hard to sit back and wait for a Dragon to make a decision on their timeline. (That impatience is your inner Dragon wanting to take over!) If Peter is slow to make a decision, I get a strong feeling of anxiety that starts in my stomach and builds in my chest; it's a mixture of impatience and frustration that, as I wait for him, makes me want to yell, "Just make a decision already!"

In relationships, a lot of Dragons remain indecisive because they have been criticized for their decisions in the past and would prefer to make no decision than a wrong one. We Tigers created that behavior, and now we need to learn to reverse it.

Start by regularly giving your Dragon the freedom to make more decisions, particularly decisions that impact both of you. It doesn't matter how small the decision is, the act of making the decisions will help fuel their self-respect and push them deeper into their Dragon energy. Meanwhile, your Tiger energy will also be stoked, because allowing them to make the decision forces you to practice surrendering, letting go, and being truly indifferent to the outcome.

I am not saying that you should sit quietly while your Dragon partner goes off and makes the decision to sell your house or move the family to another city; you are still in a relationship, after all. But in the micro-moments of your life, surrendering decision-making can be a powerful technique to fuel your Polarity. Start with easy, low-conflict decisions. You will likely build up to bigger and bigger decisions, because as you go deeper into your Tiger energy, you will also start to feel more untethered and relaxed, while your Dragon feels more empowered and purposeful. Your ability to be wild and free and to go with the flow is a super sexy gift to a Dragon. Try using the words "surprise me" more often—and mean them. You'll be amazed at how sexy your Dragon finds those two words once they learn to trust them.

Most Friday nights we take the kids out for pizza and then walk to the gelato shop for a treat. One particular night in the summer, Peter went ahead to line up for gelato while I played outside with the kids. It's an amazing, authentic Italian gelato shop with over thirty fantastic flavors. After a long wait, Peter came back with four scoops of vanilla gelato. He immediately saw the look of disappointment on my face and said, "I didn't know what flavor you wanted, so I got vanilla—it's amazing."

A more evolved Tiger who was focused on encouraging their Dragon partner to practice decision-making would have said, "Thank you, baby, I'm excited to try it." Instead I said, "Really? You don't know what flavor I wanted? We've been together for eighteen years." I then paused, looked him in the eye, and asked, "Seriously, what's my favorite flavor?" He turned away, abashed, and said, "I guess salted caramel." I had undoubtedly won the argument of the moment, but I had also successfully ruined our evening by squashing my Dragon's instincts. Let's just say there was no lovemaking that night.

What I've since learned is that it's not so bad to eat a scoop of vanilla gelato every once in a while if that means I can experience a deeper Dragon. I now try to withhold any criticism of a decision that Peter makes, especially if the results don't really matter. Instead, I'm happy that he made the decision at all. When Dragons are leading, we Tigers can relax and tag along for the fun bits. Sometimes you have to enjoy your vanilla gelato for what it is: a decision-free frozen treat.

A physical extension of decision-making is leadership, or "leading the way," which is also a physical manifestation of freedom. It might seem obvious, but by encouraging your Dragon to physically lead you, it will help push them deeper into their Dragon energy. You can let your Dragon drive the car or, if you are going for a walk/run/bike together, have your Dragon choose the path you are taking. If you are going out to dinner or a party, hold out your arm and let them physically lead you to where you are going. Or even better, if you are in the mood for intimacy, hold out your hand and ask your Dragon to lead you to the bedroom. You could even put on a blindfold so that they are forced to lead you! This might seem a little strange, but these physical acts help your Dragon to connect with their freedom and will help stoke the Dragon fire in their belly.

The thing about taking the lead and making decisions is that it requires both attention and presence. Therefore, by having your

Dragon make decisions on your behalf, you are forcing them to be present with you in the moment. And in fact, this leads to the third tool in your Dragon-fire-stoking toolbox: rewarding presence.

Reward a Dragon's Presence

One of the great gifts that a Dragon offers a Tiger is their deep consciousness. In the same way that the Dragon craves a Tiger's radiance, a Tiger craves a Dragon's presence. In order to be deeply seen and loved by your Dragon, they need to be fully present in the moment. If your Dragon isn't deep and present enough to hold the flow of your energy, then you will start to feel alone, untethered, and unseen.

Often Peter will have long periods where he is disconnected at home. He might be physically present, but he's just not that engaged with what is going on; his consciousness is elsewhere. Recently he was on a mission to buy a new car—his lease was expiring, and he needed to decide what to buy next. No matter what I did, I could not move his consciousness off that mission. When he was home, he was on his phone reading reviews, talking to his car-enthusiast friends, taking test drives, and visiting dealers. Any spare moment he had was consumed with this bloody mission. After three or four weeks of obsessing, he finally made his decision and came home with his new car. For the first time in weeks I could look him in the eye and see his full consciousness. "So great to see you again," I told him. "I missed you."

Immediately, he apologized for being absent from home and from the kids, but he said he felt great now he had that job done—"mission accomplished." My temptation, now that I finally had his attention, was to remind him of all the ways he had been absent over that past month, how frustrating it had been, and how exhausted and alone it had made me feel. I wanted to tell him that the car didn't really matter; it was a stupid waste of time, and his time was better spent with us or at work. But that would have zapped his Dragon energy and probably made him regret mentally "coming home" at all. I was happy to have him back. I didn't want him to disappear again. So instead I concentrated on rewarding him for the successful completion of a mission.

We had champagne and took the kids to the garage to check out the new car. We clapped, we laughed, we jumped up and down—we really put on a sparkle show. I then used this moment to encourage more of his presence at home. We went skateboarding with the kids, we took time to chat over a coffee, and then we made love that night. I felt seen for the first time in weeks and wanted to make sure he knew that when he brought his consciousness back to me, he would be rewarded.

Whenever your Dragon brings their consciousness home, use affirmations to ensure that they feel encouraged rather than spending that time unpacking reserved frustrations. You can (and should) still share those frustrations with your Dragon—just don't do it right at that moment. Make notes about your frustrations and share them with your Dragon at a later time when they are on solid ground and firmly back in their Dragon energy. Right now, in the moment when they have come back to you, show them through your body and your actions that you are happy to have them with you. Kiss them. Touch them. Nourish them with your Tiger love.

Show Respect

The last way you can help push your Dragon deeper into their Dragon energy is by finding ways to show them that you respect and honor them.

This means that, at any given moment, you'll need to ignore all of the things that they are fucking up (which I am sure on most days outweigh their achievements). Don't worry, you can still have your feelings of frustration and disappointment and see room for improvement, but park those feelings for the moment and instead focus on the reasons you respect your Dragon. Each day pay attention and identify something about them that you truly trust, that they do well, or that you admire or respect, and find a way of communicating that to your Dragon. If you can do it in front of others, even better.

Publicly dishing out respect goes a long way in supercharging Dragon energy. When we are out with family or friends, I use it as an opportunity to really lay it on thick. I try to steer the conversation to a topic where Peter is highly knowledgeable. I will brag about his achievements, and I share stories that demonstrate his strength. I also ensure that I repost any of his LinkedIn posts with proud comments of admiration and that I compliment him on Facebook for his accomplishments. Anything I can do to publicly show respect for his achievements will assist in fueling his inner Dragon and ensuring he feels deeply respected, admired, and honored.

Of course, not all demonstrations of respect can be public. Public or private, show respect however you can: Do it in person or via email, text message, carrier pigeon, or Morse code. . . . However you need to convey it, do it. You'll be amazed at the depths your Dragon can go to with regular affirmations.

I started by sending Peter a daily text telling him how grateful I was for the luxury of having the kids in day care and being able to write my book. As obvious as this sounds, when I send Peter a text, I intentionally use the words "respect" and "admire" in the message. I try not to write more than two sentences (if it is too long he may not read it or even fear that it is some sort of test), just a little ping on his phone to encourage him into the depths of his Dragon, something like, *"I deeply respect you for how hard you are working on that new account. Thank you for everything you do for our family."*

After a couple of weeks of sending him small notes of gratitude, there was a dramatic change in our energy dynamic. Each day Peter would come home, look me in the eye, and thank me for the message. He would tell me how much it meant to him that I acknowledged and appreciated the choice we had made to lose my income. What I didn't expect was for him to start feeding my Tiger energy right back. He started to be more present, thank me more for my love and nurturing, give me unexpected gifts, and comment on how pretty I looked. Needless to say, our lovemaking also leveled up a notch.

By me feeding Peter a little respect, he started to see me and feed me more love. It was literally a win-win and proof that even the smallest efforts toward Polarity can produce very real—and very welcome—results.

CHAPTER 12

Navigating Past Neutral

After moving into his Dragon (and before I moved into my Tiger), Peter had decided that we were both Dragons and that the primary purposes of our marriage were friendship, family, and business. He decided, unilaterally (and unconsciously), that I was too set in my ways to change, and that it would be impossible to get what he needed from me sexually. As a result, he sought passion from other relationships. I too had decided that the primary purpose of our relationship was friendship and financial success, and while I didn't seek intimacy outside our relationship, I just learned to live without it.

We were stuck in neutral with no Polarity to create a spark.

Perhaps after reading the book so far, you have identified yourself and your partner as being energetically the same. That is, you are both dominant Tigers, both dominant Dragons, or you're both 50 percent Tiger and 50 percent Dragon (while that's rare, it does happen). We're talking about energy, after all, and there are no hard-and-fast rules about how you energetically exist or relate to your partner. However, before you set your view in stone, I would encourage you to chat about this topic with your partner and see what they think. They may be a closeted Dragon or Tiger repressing their energy for the perceived sake of the relationship.

If you are making a unilateral decision on behalf of your partner, I encourage you to use the following techniques to work on the problem together, even if it feels impossible. You might be amazed by what you are both capable of.

Prioritizing Polarity

If you are in neutral energy territory, I am sure you already feel the lack of attraction between you and your partner. It's important that you are deeply honest about what you want from your primary relationship. Do you need deep passion? Or are you happy with a lifelong friendship, a balanced co-parent, or a financial beneficiary?

It is important that you and your partner are on the same page and are deeply honest about what you want. If you want the purpose of your primary relationship to be an intimate and sexually satisfying relationship, then you need to make that a priority. That doesn't mean you can't and won't also be financial partners, best friends, or co-parents—it means you elevate one pillar above the others.

With painful openness and honesty, Peter and I have both agreed that we want and require the stability of monogamy, which means that prioritizing our sexual relationship is critical because it is the one area of our lives we need each other for and can't fulfill outside of our marriage. I can have other business partners, deep friendships, and find my own financial satisfaction and freedom, but I need Peter for intimacy and to feel truly satisfied.

If you have the same Dominant Energy as your partner and you also want to have Polarity in your romantic relationship, then it will need to become a priority, and one (or both) of you is going to have to learn to shift your energy from time to time to create some heat. And if you are the one reading this book, there's a pretty good chance it will need to be you.

If you and your partner are both Dragons, then you can use the techniques presented in the previous chapters to push your partner even deeper into their Dragon energy while you temporarily relax into your Tiger energy. Likewise, if both you and your partner are Tigers, then you may need to ground your inner Dragon from time to time to create some space.

You don't always need to be poles apart, but pushing into them from time to time will help to keep the spark alive. You don't want to spend too long out of your Dominant Energy or you will feel drained; stay there just long enough to create a little heat. The more fun you have with it, the better your chances of success.

PART IV

ACTION STEPS

How to Create Polarity

As you hopefully see by now, you don't need to wait for a vacation to find Polarity. You can learn how to encourage your partner to go deeper into their Dominant Energy right now. This is the fun part, the part where you go out into the wild and try a few of these techniques.

DRAGONS

To help your partner to embody their Tiger energy:

1. Ensure your partner feels safe. That sense of safety comes from many micro-moments, not just the big ones. Consistently do what you say you are going to do so they know they can rely on you no matter what.

2. Lead your partner from their mind into their body. Lead them from their "doing" into their "feeling" with your presence and depth of consciousness.

3. Reward feelings and pleasure with your full attention and consciousness. Make sure your partner knows how much you love it when they shine.

4. Take the Dragon Throne. Stay there and draw out the inner Tiger. It might take fifteen minutes or it might take two days, but continue to claim the throne and watch as your partner relaxes into their Tiger.

TIGERS

To help your partner go deep into their Dragon energy:

1. Support your partner to fulfill their current purpose. If they don't have one, help them find it.

2. Give your Dragon the freedom to make more decisions. It doesn't matter how small the decision is: The mere act of making decisions will help fuel their self-respect.

3. Reward presence. Whenever your Dragon brings their consciousness home, show them through your words, your body, and your actions that you are happy to have them with you. Kiss them, touch them, and nourish them with your Tiger love.

4. Find ways to show them that you respect and honor them. Whether you do it privately or publicly, ensure that your Dragon knows they are respected.

Remember, your partner may be concealing their deep energetic cravings from you, particularly if they don't think you are capable of giving them what they need. So talk about it. Work on it together.

PUSHING YOUR PARTNER AWAY TO CREATE ATTRACTION

The checklists here provide a number of ideas for creating more Polarity with your partner. If it feels intimidating, my best advice is to start with something small. Find the thing about your counterpart that you do believe in, and work on encouraging that trait in them. I encourage you to journal the experiment and monitor the changes.

As you begin the process, you may need to fake it a little, but it will be worth it. If you're a Tiger, some days you'll need to show your Dragon respect when you don't think they deserve it; if you're a Dragon, you may need to shower your Tiger with affection and consciousness even if you don't feel like it. In these cases, what you're doing will probably feel a little contrived and ingenuine. That's okay. Stick with it and you'll find the energy dynamics slowly starting to shift.

PART V

Poisoning Polarity

Despite our good intentions, there are three recurring areas where Peter and I keep messing up our Polarity: how we want to be supported when we are *stressed*, how and when we are prepared for great *sex*, and how we handle *money*.

Stress. Sex. Money. When it comes to these three themes, Tigers and Dragons couldn't be further apart in their thinking and feelings. In times of stress and in our approach to sex and money, we tend to make the same mistakes with each other time and time again—rapidly unraveling all of the hard work we've done to build love, trust, respect, and desire.

For the most part we approach these areas of our lives with the best intentions. But while our intentions might be good, our actions weaken the foundation of our relationship rather than reinforce it.

During a stressful time, failing to deliver what our partner needs can make them feel as if they have been abandoned and misunderstood. Failing to meet each other's sexual needs can result in infidelity, excessive self-pleasure, sexual deprivation, or repression. And our differing attitudes toward finances can lead to feeling disrespected, resented, unappreciated, and unloved.

These are the three areas where Peter and I continue to struggle the most. Despite our awareness of these triggers, we still slip back into old energetic patterns of behavior. Essentially we are a work in progress; through intention and open communication we have made strides over time. By improving (if not mastering) these recurring challenges, we find it much easier to keep our attraction flowing.

The trouble is that we approach these areas by trying to give our partner what *we* think they need, which comes from our own energy and is usually the opposite of what they actually need. The key is learning to provide a polar opposite partner with what *they* need rather than what *you* need.

CHAPTER 13

Stress

The unfortunate reality is that when our partner is stressed, going through trauma, or faced with a challenge, that is when we tend to do the most (unintentional) damage. This chapter is going to try to reverse that. And the first step is understanding what your partner needs during this tumultuous time.

When a Dragon is stressed or faced with a problem, their natural response is to seek solitude in order to try to solve the problem independently and rationally. The only time a Dragon wants to openly talk about a problem with someone else is when they believe that person can offer specialized insight that will help them solve the problem. The only exception is if they feel they need to explain that they didn't cause the problem; if a village is on fire, given that they are a fire-breathing Dragon, they may want to talk to let the villagers know that they didn't start the fire. Otherwise, they are only going to talk to the fire department about putting it out. Most of all, what a Dragon wants is to get a problem fixed.

Tigers have a hard time sitting back, biting their lip, and watching a Dragon work through their problem alone. Because, when a Tiger has a problem or feels stressed, they want to talk to *everyone* about it. If there's a village fire, they want to talk to the Dragon, the fire department, the villagers, the neighboring villagers; hell, they'll escalate this all the way to the queen if they have to. The Tiger won't just examine the issue that is before them; after twenty minutes of talking, the Tiger will likely have taken this problem to extremes the Dragon didn't even know were possible.

For the Tiger, at this moment, stress doesn't need to be "fixed," but it needs to be "felt." Tigers expand and share their problems in order to feel them all the way through to rupture and closure. That process is not linear. By exploring their feelings through this process, the Tiger gains a greater awareness of what is really bothering them, and then, suddenly, like a popped balloon, they will no longer feel so overwhelmed. But it is a painful process for the Dragon to watch.

With all that in mind, let's see what we can do to help each other out in times of stress.

Dragons, Stop Walking Away from a Stressed Tiger

Dragons, when you are faced with a Tiger who is stressed, experiencing trauma, or in a crisis, there are two things that you need to stop doing: First, you need to stop giving them space by walking away. Second, when you do stay and stand firm, you need to resist the temptation to solve the problem for them.

When your Tiger partner is stressed and talking endlessly about a problem, your subconscious Dragon impulse will always be to walk away. After all, Dragons like to be alone when they are upset or trying to solve a problem. But remember, you are not dealing with another Dragon now; you are dealing with a Tiger, and Tigers want company. They want to make things bigger—to talk about them, share them, and fill up and expand issues to a point where they rupture before they calm down. So stay present, watch the storm build, and be there to pick up the pieces when it passes—and it will. If you weather the storm from start to finish, you may never have to witness that particular storm again. Oh, there will be others, but if you let a storm take its full course, next time it will not be as big.

What you probably don't realize is that when you walk away from a Tiger storm, you are actually forcing your Tiger into their Dragon energy at the precise moment when they have an opportunity to really *let go* and dive deeper into their Tiger energy. You are poisoning Polarity by leaving them alone to fend for themselves; by walking away you are telling your Tiger to be more like a Dragon, instead of embracing their Tiger wildness. Stand firm. Be the Dragon.

Now that you are standing firm (and I know this is going to be hard), as you see your Tiger partner expanding their problems, resist the temptation to try to solve those problems for them. I am sure you can see the issue clearly; I am sure your solution is simple and effective. But this is a *feeling* process for the Tiger, not a *thinking* process. So instead of being bothered by the fact that your Tiger doesn't want to hear about or has rejected your awesome solution and instead of taking it personally, I encourage you to forget you are even watching a human and instead imagine you are marveling at a tropical storm.

Watch the energy, not the person. Watch as the pressure builds up in the storm, as it gets upgraded to a hurricane; then watch it go from a category 1 to a category 2, then 3, 4, and 5. Watch the storm in all of its unpredictable, beautiful, wild glory as it moves around you. Disengage from the storm. This storm is not your doing, and it certainly isn't your job to *fix* it. It is your job to *weather* it and be there after it passes to help clean up the mess. It's wild, destructive, and absolutely captivating.

Standing firm and weathering a Tiger storm will not only make your Tiger feel safe to let go and feel the problem through to its rupture, but it will also help ground you deeper into your Dragon energy (which, in turn, will create more sexual space between you). There's a reason "make-up sex" is a thing. But you only have great make-up sex if you are still standing in the room at the end of the storm.

Peter has learned to stand firm, even if I tell him to leave or slam the door in his face. He will put his nose to the door and say, "You can't push me away. I'm not going anywhere. I want to be here." And then he will wait it out. Depending on how wild I get, I will continue to do things to try to push him away, to test his commitment and depth. I will say horrible things designed to hurt him, but he will say, "That's really hurtful, but I know you don't mean it," and again he will repeat, "I'm not going anywhere."

We have had some pretty big fights over the years, but through his consistency, I have learned to trust him again despite everything we have been through. What I have found is that knowing he is going to weather the storm automatically downgrades it for me. My storms now rarely ratchet up to a category 5.

Tigers, Don't Intrude in the Dragon's Den of Solitude

Tigers, you are highly intuitive and can easily sense when your Dragon partner has a problem or is stressed, likely because they have withdrawn into their den of solitude. (The silence can be deafening.) I know this is going to be hard, but you need to resist the temptation to follow your Dragon into their den.

Your Dragon partner loves you and really doesn't want to be rude. If you chase them into their den of solitude and insist that they share what is going on, they will more than likely oblige you, even though you are neither a firefighter nor a villager. And after your Dragon has shared the problem, you will be tempted to do what you do best: talk. And talk. And talk some more. But a Dragon doesn't want their problem to expand, and they don't want to feel it through; they want their problem to go away. And now they want you to go away, too.

If your Dragon wants your help solving their problem, they will ask for it. When you ideate the problem for them, the Dragon perceives that as you offering unsolicited advice, which will make them feel as if you do not believe that they have the ability to solve that problem on their own. When you workshop the problem without being asked to, your Dragon partner views that as you increasing your own Dragon energy and pushing them into their Tiger—thereby poisoning your Polarity. I promise you, there will be no sexual attraction in the moments that follow your unsolicited advice—as awesome as your advice may be.

As a formerly dominant Dragon business owner and executive, I find it really hard to step back. I was paid a lot of money to solve problems and improve efficiencies. But now, if I can sense that Peter has a problem, I will gently ask him if he wants to share it. If he does, then I try to listen with an open heart full of love and resist the temptation to help solve his problem. When he eventually pauses and looks to me for my response, I will ask him what he needs from me at this moment. If he says, "Nothing, really," then I just focus on opening my heart wider and shining love into the moment. Alternatively, if he confirms that he wants my insights, I provide them.

Dragons want solitude, and they want to feel as if they solved their problems unassisted. This is a form of freedom. As hard as it is, let your Dragon solve their own problems. Bring your Tiger energy to the situation by feeling it, rather than processing it. That is your Tiger gift to give to your Dragon, and that is what the Dragon craves. Be present and conscious, open your heart, and offer your love to the moment. Be the Tiger.

Using Polarity to Ease Stress

For the most part, our innate reactions to the stress that our partners face make the situation worse, not better. Dragons walk away from stressed Tigers, which increases the Tiger's feeling of abandonment and isolation. Tigers intrude on Dragon's solitude, which escalates the tension.

When your partner is stressed, let them deal with it in their own way while you remain firm in your energy. By being present with their steady energy, Dragons can help the Tiger's storm pass more quickly. By focusing on letting their love shine through, Tigers can provide a steady light into a Dragon's den without intruding. Embracing our own energy and respecting our partner's opposite energy won't eliminate stress from our lives, but it can lessen the impact on our relationships.

CHAPTER 14

Money

Oh, money.

Money. Money. Money. (Audible sigh.)

This part of the book was written and included at Peter's express request. My attitude to money created so much confusion, conflict, and resentment in our relationship that Peter wanted me to dedicate an entire chapter to it. And now that I more fully understand the opposite ways in which Dragons and Tigers think about and use money, I have to agree with him.

Whether you have a lot or a little, money is a major hot spot for Dragons and Tigers. In short, we decimate our Polarity by disrespecting each other's view of money, its value, and its purpose. Just look at the animal energy totems: Dragons are frequently portrayed living in caves, fiercely protecting piles of treasure. Meanwhile, what on earth would a Tiger want with a gold coin?

Our current capitalist, consumer-driven society trains us to believe that money is the ultimate measure of success. And Dragons buy in. Most Dragons believe that they will be happy when they have enough money; it is the ultimate phantom freedom. Money is a very simple way for competitive Dragons to objectively keep score.

After meeting someone new, Peter will say, "I've got his number." To Peter that means he believes he knows what the person is earning, whether Peter is earning more or less, and whether he has financial inferiority or superiority. I, on the other hand, will comment on whether I "clicked" with the new person. I'm interested in my gut feeling as to whether we will be friends, not how much money either of us makes.

For deep Tiger energy, money is a tool to be used to help a Tiger feel seen and loved, as well as a way to show those in their lives that they care for them. Money comes in, money goes out; money isn't a measure or an anchor for the Tiger, but rather just another man-made thing. The Tiger values money as a way to express their self-love and love for others, using it to buy considerate gifts and experiences. Money allows a Tiger to deeply express their love and thoughtfulness and to help nourish the lives of those who see and love them in return. And when Dragons don't see money the same way, well, that's why we have a whole chapter on this relationship killer.

Dragons, Stop Keeping Score

I have some news for you, Dragons. While you might use money to keep score with other Dragons, this type of scoring system really doesn't work when it comes to loving a Tiger. One dollar doesn't equal one emotional love point for your Tiger. To a Tiger, any act of love or gift that makes them feel seen and valued is equally important, irrelevant of its value.

Let me put this in Dragon-scoring language: Buying your Tiger a car worth $100,000 doesn't make them feel 2,000 times more loved than buying them a bunch of flowers or a bottle of wine for $50.

Tigers don't keep score like that. And I can say this with authority, because it's an exact circumstance that arose in my relationship.

One recent December, Peter made plans to pre-order me a new car. He set aside the deposit money and was going to take me in to "build" the car in January. Because of this plan, he told me he wasn't buying me anything for Christmas. His reasoning was sound, yet I didn't really believe him. In my mind, what he meant was he wouldn't be getting me a "big" Christmas present. On Christmas Day, when everyone opened their gifts, I realized there really wasn't a gift under the tree for me. Despite Peter's having clearly communicated his rationale and intentions, I was sad and disappointed. I knew a bigger gift was coming, but my feelings couldn't move past the present moment; I didn't feel loved or appreciated at all.

Peter, Dragon that he is, was both confused and angered by my reaction. In his mind he had done everything right: He had organized the big gift, he'd been honest with me about Christmas, and now he thought I was acting like a spoiled child. But I couldn't help how I *felt*.

Because Dragons believe that they will score big for big things and score less for little things, they focus their time, energy, and effort into doing big things. But really, a massage, a dance, a compliment, or a box of baked goods all show a Tiger that you care in equal measure to a new car. When you expect your Tiger to *think* about money instead of *feeling* the joys that money can deliver, you are pushing your Tiger into their logical Dragon. And we know exactly what that does for Polarity.

So when you feel yourself starting to financially keep score, make a concerted effort to give your partner love and attention each day instead. (Especially during holidays or other gift-giving occasions.) You can do the big things, but don't think doing two big things a year will make your Tiger feel loved—you have to keep doing the small stuff too. It's simply the Tiger love currency; you can't fight it.

Tigers, Stop Disrespecting Boundaries

This can be hard to admit, but we Tigers tend to allow our feelings to outweigh our logic when it comes to finances. And this perplexes and frustrates the Dragon.

Money is a way in which Dragons measure their worth. Therefore, when your Dragon perceives that you disrespect their money or your shared money, they perceive that you disrespect them. Breaking budgets and spending on frivolous items can drive the Dragon to believe you don't value them. In fact, if you are trying to hurt a Dragon, money is a great place to start. One of the first things I did when I discovered Peter's infidelity was to go on a spending spree. It was the easiest and fastest way for me to hurt him.

Even though I no longer want to hurt Peter (in fact I want the very opposite), respecting financial boundaries continues to be a recurring challenge for me. As irrational as it sounds, for a long time I felt as if his income was "ours," but my income was "mine." Peter and I set financial goals, created spending limits, and agreed to family financial boundaries, but I regularly became impulsive, broke the rules, and spent "my money" however I pleased—on a sale I walk past, a new plant for the house, a laser treatment session, or a gift for a friend. When I did manage to show enough restraint to withhold from impulsive spending, I then (unconsciously) found myself slowly and methodically making Peter feel guilty about my clear deprivation of indulgence. I would continue to subtly (and not so subtly) complain until he agreed to change the boundary.

When and if Peter finally agreed to change the boundary, he felt disappointed in himself for not being stronger, and he became resentful of me for putting him in that position and disrespecting our boundaries in the first place. If I injured him deeply enough, I poisoned our Polarity by pushing him out of his Dragon altogether and into his Tiger energy, where he would start to question the point of it all. In his worst Tiger moments he would lose control, and we would head out on an emotional Tiger shopping spree. But the joy was short-lived, because when the energy settled, Peter's self-loathing and shame started to close in.

We have now (mostly) broken this cycle by having a monthly amount that provides for my emotional needs. It's a small discretionary amount that I can use however I like. Oddly enough, I rarely use it, but knowing it is there makes me feel more emotionally free and less suffocated by his fiscal controls. And it solves the issue of my wheedling over or ignoring our financial boundaries, because this wiggle room is built in.

Even if you can't build a small discretionary fund into your budget, there are other solutions. For instance, when you feel yourself about to overstep a financial boundary, consider if there is another way you can satisfy your current emotional need. Would a heartfelt letter to a friend be just as powerful as a gift? Would an after-dinner gelato stroll be just as effective as a three-course restaurant meal? I know that since I stopped overstepping and started respecting our financial boundaries, we have had far less conflict and resentment in our relationship. I deeply respect Peter for standing firm and for his commitment to our long-term financial security, which further feeds my trust in him and his depth as a Dragon. And there's something very sexy about that.

When it comes to money, *increasing* Polarity may not be a goal as it is in other areas. But by *adapting* to Dragon/Tiger differences, you can reduce the chance that money-related tension and stress will interfere with positive Polarity with your partner.

CHAPTER 15

Sex

In Parts VI and VII, I am going to shift gears and start to discuss how our Tiger/Dragon energy can impact other areas of our life, like our relationship with our family and our performance at work. Therefore it is only fitting that, in this last chapter focused on romantic relationships, we should bring it home with a frank discussion of sex.

Deep down we all want to experience wild, passionate, exceptional sex. I don't care how sexually liberal or conservative you are—great sex is, well . . . great. For most of us, having great sex is pretty easy at the beginning of a relationship. Our natural love hormones create a beautiful cocktail that makes it all very lustful and exciting. But after that, if monogamy is important and we still want to have great sex, what can we do?

If you haven't caught on by now, essentially every lesson and insight provided in this book so far has been a foundational tool to help you enjoy more desire and passion with your partner. This is not about putting lipstick on a pig; this is about transforming your entire energy interaction in such a way that you and your partner no longer look like pigs at all, but rather sizzling pieces of bacon. (Apologies to the vegans out there, but come on—it's bacon!)

Driving Your Ferrari Like a Minivan

For over a decade, Peter and I enjoyed regular sex and it was pretty good—it certainly checked the box. Peter didn't look like a sizzling piece of bacon, but he was a respectable slice of baked ham. But because we were both in our Dragon energy, it was all very practical, almost clinical. To avoid feeling like friends, we both knew it was important to stay physically connected, so we "got it done." But our sex was missing *heart*. It lacked the depth of connection that Polarity brings; it was missing the wild, free, ethereal Tiger energy. Someone needs to be the *devourer*, and someone needs to be the *devouree*.

During sex, we have a very special and important opportunity to return to the source, to feel whole and to be "one." We have the opportunity to stop being friends, two separate beings, and disappear into each other: for Dragons to feel free and for Tigers to feel seen and loved. We have the opportunity to feel authentically happy and whole.

Don't get me wrong. Sex can be physiological and functional—and there is a time and place for that. But having functional sex is like owning a Ferrari and never driving it over 50 mph. It turns out that for that decade I was driving my Ferrari like a Goddamned minivan, just shuttling it around town to pick up the groceries and dry cleaning. What a waste!

In the same way that the Ferrari engine begs to be opened up, so does the Tiger heart. It wants to be cracked open, seen, desired, and devoured by the present, grounded Dragon. And there is nothing more attractive to the Dragon than a Tiger who lets go and truly surrenders their body and opens their heart for devouring. Practically, phrases like "take me" will often do the trick.

And there is nothing more desirable to the Tiger than a Dragon who then confidently takes the wheel and leads the Tiger from their head (*thinking*) to their body (*feeling*) all the way through to their pleasure. When the Dragon connects with the Tiger in body and soul, the Dragon feels free. And if Tigers can do this for their Dragon, they will burn down entire villages for that pleasure.

I know what you're thinking: *That's all good and well, but how do I do that? How do I find the time and space to connect in a deep and meaningful way?* Well, I'm glad you asked. Because it all starts with preparation. In fact, it starts long before you actually want to connect.

There are things that we all do during the immediate lead-up to sex that can decimate desire. And while it might seem obvious by this stage in the book (and life), the first thing you need to do is to stop assuming your partner approaches sex the same way you do. They are not you, and thank the heavens for that—you would never be attracted to yourself, because you would have no Polarity!

With that in mind, let's help each other out.

Dragons, Stop Rejecting Your Tiger

My Dragons, it is important for you to realize that, unlike you, Tigers need time to mentally prepare to open. You have a tendency to physically and emotionally disappear while you're working on your current purpose, and then when you're ready, you'll pop out of your den of solitude (usually after solving a problem or making progress on your mission), and all of a sudden you're ready to celebrate . . . with sex.

The bad news is that if you unintentionally spurned or emotionally injured your Tiger while you were possessed by your purpose in your den of solitude, then you will have a little work to do before "great sex" is on the table.

While you were off on your mission, a couple of things might have happened: (1) Your Tiger was in the mood, failed to capture your attention, and is now feeling rejected, or (2) Your Tiger got tired of waiting around and therefore made other plans.

If your Tiger did try to intrude into your den of solitude to capture your attention, in all likelihood you (unintentionally) rejected them and made them feel unseen and unloved. This can be frustrating for the Dragon, because it may feel as if your Tiger always waits for the worst possible time to desire sex; it's as if they wait until you are clearly on an important mission to come at you. Well, guess what: When you are grounded and full of purpose, that is when you are the most attractive to your Tiger. That is when they will want to play a game of catch and release with you to tempt you and distract you away from your mission. Instead of being frustrated by your Tiger for their terrible timing, see it for what it is: Your Tiger is seducing you. Enjoy it!

If you don't want to take a break or you can't because you are on a mission, try not to injure your Tiger with rejection. Instead, make plans. Explain to the Tiger that you are on a deadline and in the flow and that as much as you love them and are attracted to their open heart and their body full of pleasure, you need to delay that pleasure a little longer. Set a time and a place, and commit to that. Once you have committed, it is important to follow through with your commitment, because that will continue to build trust and desire.

Now if your Tiger still gets injured by your rejection, it will be important to reward the Tiger with your presence and deep consciousness when it is time to reconnect. You must allow them to vent and feel it all through. Let them storm if they need to (see Chapter 13), and then be there for the make-up sex at the end.

The second possibility is that while you were hyper-focusing off in your den of solitude, your Tiger got tired of waiting and so made other plans. They might even have gone back into their Dragon to "get stuff done." The good news is that now you have a new mission: to have sex with your Tiger. In order to achieve your mission, you will need to give your Tiger some time to get out of their Dragon skin and back into their Tiger so they can feel your Polarity again. The tools in Chapter 10 will help you with that.

In any and all of these situations, keep in mind that your Tiger may not be mentally ready for sex in a quick Dragon second. Sometimes the Tiger needs to feel that they are worthy of being seen and desired. It can be really hard for a Tiger to feel desirable when they feel unkempt, out of shape, or grimy from the day. Most Tigers will need space and time to get themselves physically and mentally prepared for sex.

I speak from personal experience here. Peter and I enjoy date night every Saturday night. No one else is invited; it's just the two of us connecting. There is a clear expectation, set by Peter, that we will have sex on date night. Because I know this going in, I am mentally prepared. No matter how deep I am pulled into my Dragon during the week, before every date night I follow a preparation ritual. I take at least an hour to get ready, sometimes two or three (seriously!); I take a long shower or bath; and I shave my legs, do my hair, moisturize, tweeze, carefully apply my makeup, and change outfits several times, all while listening to music and taking intermittent breaks to dance half naked in the living room with the girls.

This lengthy ritual allows me to feel relaxed and happy and is a critical part of shedding my Dragon skin and stepping into my pleasure-filled Tiger. It allows me to connect with my physical self and feel beautiful and lovable. It taps into my need to feel seen and desired and my ability to be open to pleasure. When Peter rushes that, my deep pleasure turns into anger and anxiety. It pushes me into my Dragon, and it decreases my ability to enjoy the evening. If we skip this step, we also usually skip sex after dinner.

Put in the work to understand what your Tiger needs to feel prepared for intimate time with you. Ask them. Communicate. You can share your desire to connect with them, but then you need to move mountains to make sure they get what they need. This is your mission. It won't feel spontaneous, but it will feel great.

Tigers, Don't Expect Your Dragon to Anticipate Your Needs

Tigers, when it comes to enjoying intimacy, timing really is everything, isn't it? And sometimes it feels like trying to align the stars—either you aren't in the mood when your partner is, or you are ready to get down but your Dragon is a million miles away (physically or metaphorically).

The ultimate goal is to create the perfect amount of sexual tension so that you meet your partner at the right place, at the right time, so you can have wild, passionate sex. You want the kind of sex that feels spiritual and demands a postcoital high five. (Surely I am not the only one who does that after great sex.)

Is that too much to ask for?

But of course sometimes you just aren't "feeling it." I get that. Yet your need to "feel it" can get in the way of your having great sex!

Take a moment to deeply consider what it is you need in order to "feel it." Is there a magic formula that is sure to work every time? If not (and I can almost guarantee there is not), stop expecting your Dragon partner to know what it is you need to *feel* ready for intimacy. This is not something your Dragon is going to be able to anticipate.

For me, I know that I need to feel beautiful, feel appreciated, and feel as if I am desirable. When Peter rolls over in the morning and pushes his morning glory into my back, I don't feel any of those things. I feel groggy because I was up three times with a potty-training toddler, my breath stinks, my hair is feral, and I'm anxious one of the kids will walk in and bust us. Sex in this type of environment makes me feel like a means to an end. And if I have sex in that environment, I know I am not going to be able to enjoy myself. Afterward, my heart will be sad, and I will feel used.

It took time, but eventually I was able to analyze my reactions and share my feelings with Peter. I was able to explain to him that feeling seen and connected was critical for me to enjoy sex. It's also important that I am not in the middle of doing something—that is, I cannot be in my Dragon mode. I need to be in a place where I have shed my Dragon skin and am not thinking of the million other things that I need to do. The reality is that I still spend a lot of time in my Dragon. The kids force me there, my work forces me there, society forces me there! As much as I try to live my life in my dominant Tiger, I still get drawn into my Dragon. A lot.

Through our discussions and through practice, Peter now knows that I need my time and space to feel beautiful and desirable. On our first few date nights, Peter did his best to give me space and time to get ready, but he would still storm the bathroom doorway and rush me because we were going to be late. Yet when I walked out of the bathroom at 1,000 mph, I got hugely frustrated and disappointed to see that the basic things that needed to be done around the house weren't done.

What Tigers forget is that Dragons actually love purpose—they love to be needed. So start explaining to your Dragon what you need from them. Give them a mission. If your Dragon knows this will translate to great sex, sit back and watch them swoop in and help you.

I can already visualize your eyes rolling. I know you think it's not that simple, because you have been disappointed in the past.

But I encourage you to try again, this time using your open heart. It is frustrating for Tigers, who are naturally intuitive, to ask for help with tasks. We tend to think, "I shouldn't have to ask; it is clear that these things need to be done. If you loved me you would notice, and you would help me." Well, Dragons aren't naturally intuitive, so they aren't going to see things this way. Therefore it's on you to suck it up and learn to expressly ask for help.

Now, instead of being overwhelmed by all of the things I need to do in order to get my ass out the door by 6 p.m., I have asked Peter for assistance, and I have given him a mission. When I blast out of the bathroom in my beautiful Tiger glory, the pizza is ordered for the kids, the sitter has been shown through the house, the address of the restaurant is loaded into his phone, the car is running, and my favorite song is playing on the car stereo (seriously). When I see all of this, I physically exhale and look at him with complete lust. This is a Dragon leading me, in control. Our night is infinitely more intimate and enjoyable because I can now trust that he has everything in hand, and I can relax into my Tiger.

So that's all about getting *yourself* into the mood for some lovin'. Sometimes, however, it's your Dragon partner who's not in the mood. In these instances, you need to ask this: Are they uninterested because they are feeling lost and struggling to find their purpose, their edge, and their depth? Or are they uninterested in sex because they are busy "doing"?

If it's the former, they could be having themselves a Tiger moment. If that is the case, I encourage you to take this opportunity to just roll with it and try going deeper into your own Dragon energy. Try to physically lead them, be strong, make decisions . . . sexually dominate. Have fun and play into the temporary energy inversion. If that fails to do the trick, I encourage you to revisit the tools in Chapter 11 that you can use to encourage your partner back into their Dragon skin.

Now, if the problem is the latter—your Dragon isn't interested because their focus is on a mission and they are in their den of solitude solving a problem—then you'll need a slightly different approach. The good news is that being on a mission means they are deep in their Dragon; this is likely why you are finding yourself attracted to them and feeling the desire to capture their attention. I encourage you not to get frustrated or to feel rejected or hurt, but to continue to stay open and be in your Tiger.

Sometimes Peter will be working on a matter, and I will try to get his attention. When he continues to ignore me, I will find myself picking at him. I start reminding him of a bill he didn't pay or that he didn't get the dry cleaning or call his mother for her birthday. Peter will finally emerge defensively, asking, "Why are you so angry? What did I do wrong?" and I will say, "You didn't *do* anything. You are so caught up in your client matter that you are ignoring your family!"

This is my injured and ignored Tiger trying to get Peter's attention in any way I can. And picking an argument is not an elegant or sexy solution, but it will usually do the trick. Of course, it often will also start a fight—which nine times out of ten leads to the opposite outcome from what I actually wanted, which was sex.

Instead, I now try to bring my open heart to the edge of his focus. I will try to feel pleasure in my body and bring that pleasure-filled energy to Peter. I will sit quietly in the same room and touch my body, perhaps by moisturizing, stretching, and doing a little yoga, or I will do something else near him that brings me joy, like baking or drinking wine (or both at the same time). While I go about my pleasure, I try to open my heart and imagine that I am filling up the room with my light. I visualize the light moving from my sacral area (the area below the belly button) up to my heart and then gradually filling up every corner of the room. It might take a few minutes to get Peter's attention, or it might take an hour. But when I stay with it, it virtually always works.

I assure you, the Dragon feels the pleasure-filled Tiger energy in the room and is drawn to it. Your pleasure will be way more interesting than their current mission—that I promise you. And if the Dragon isn't drawn to you because they remain focused on their mission, at least you were able to fill up with a different kind of pleasure in the meantime.

Sex Is Important

I don't want to alarm you, but I do want you to take this very seriously. If you take nothing else away from this book, feel a sense of urgency around your need for a deep, authentic, sexual connection with your partner. If you are not connecting sexually, if you are in a funk or a rut, I encourage you to do the work and find a way to turn that around.

Our desire to feel whole is real, and the universe has a funny way of opening pathways for that style of connection. And if it is not happening between you and your partner, it will likely happen with someone else (sooner or later).

While you're busy, don't let someone else take your Ferrari for a spin.

Stop Poisoning Polarity

Prior to understanding our different approach to stress, money, and sex, I used to refer to Peter as my "fair-weather friend." It felt as if when I truly needed him, he just wasn't there for me. When I was stressed, he would give me space; when I was enjoying my shopping indulgences, I felt judged and criticized; and the only times that I felt sexually desired were when *he* was ready to connect (usually on vacation). Peter, naturally, is super sensitive about the term "fair-weather friend" and got angry and defensive whenever I used it. He didn't see himself as a fair-weather friend; he was treating me the way he would expect to be treated in those situations. In other words, he was treating me like a Dragon.

Thanks to all of our Polarity work, I now understand what was happening, and I can also see why he was so confused. After all, I spent most of my adult life in my Dragon energy, but whenever stress, money, or sex were involved, I reverted to my dominant Tiger. He thought I was like him in every way, when in reality I was not. We tend to give our partner what we *think* they need, which is usually the opposite of what they actually need. So that's what the previous chapters have been all about: identifying your partner's true needs and then fulfilling them.

Here are a few takeaways to help you support your partner with what they need:

DRAGONS

- Stop walking away when you are faced with a Tiger who is stressed, experiencing trauma, or in a crisis. Instead, stand firm, watch the storm pass, and be there to help pick up the pieces after it does.

- Stop trying to solve your Tiger's problems for them. The Tiger doesn't want you to "fix it," but the Tiger wants to "feel it."

- Stop using money to keep emotional "score." One dollar doesn't equal one emotional love point for your Tiger. Any act of love or gift that makes your Tiger feel seen and valued is equally important, regardless of the value.

- Stop ignoring and rejecting the Tiger when you are preoccupied with your mission. If your Tiger tries to seduce you and you can't break away, set a time and a place to reconnect and then commit to that.

- Take the time to understand what your Tiger needs to feel prepared for intimate time with you.

TIGERS

- When your Dragon is stressed or in crisis, stop following them into their den of solitude. If your Dragon wants your help solving their problem, they will ask for it.

- Bring your Tiger energy to the stressful situation by feeling it, rather than processing it. Be present and conscious, open your heart, and offer your love to the moment.

- Stop disrespecting financial boundaries. When you disrespect your Dragon's money, you disrespect the Dragon.

- Try to find ways to satisfy your desire for pleasure that don't involve spending money. It takes a little thought and creativity, but it can do wonders for your relationship!

- Take a moment to consider what it is you need in order to feel ready for intimacy. Your partner won't be able to provide you with what you need if you can't articulate it. Once you know what it is that you want and need, start to share that with your Dragon. Give them a mission.

PART VI

Family Dynamics

To start, I want to make it clear that I love my family (especially you, Mom). And I love spending time with each individual family member. I cherish having a cup of tea with my mom, a glass of champagne with my dad, and a chat with my big brother. (Here comes the "but" . . .)

But I fucking hate spending time with the four of us together. It is horrible. Toxic. Traumatic. It's no surprise that we don't get together all that often. We save the pain for the big, important holidays.

I truly have a visceral reaction to the mere thought of a family gathering. My heart feels heavy, I get a pain in my chest, and my shoulders feel tense. No matter how hard we try, no matter how good our intentions are, no matter how much we miss one another, or how desperate we all are for our social time together to be a positive experience, it just isn't. It's the worst. Something happens to us when we all come together in a room; we change and take an ugly energetic form. As much as we have all evolved as individuals, we simply regress when we get together.

When you come together as a family, there is a hierarchy, a communication style, and an energy balance. Some families get together and take on the collective Tiger energy: loving, nurturing, and pleasure-filled. Other families, like mine, take on a collective Dragon energy full of challenge, aggression, and conflict.

Like our own energy, the permutations of each family are unique. No two families are the same, and no two individuals within the same family have the same familial experience. For instance, my experience of our family unit is completely different from the experiences of my brother. (Saying that, we both agree that it isn't positive for either of us.)

Since I was already on a self-improvement journey, armed with my new Tiger-Dragon energy insights, I figured I'd take a crack at trying to improve my family interactions as well. The good news is that I did make some progress. The bad news is that it was hard, and it was slow.

When I compare my own personal change journey to the changes of my extended family unit, I liken my evolution to a speedboat—I am a single operator, and I am fast and nimble. I am cruising down the French Riviera with the wind blowing in my hair. At any time I can quickly change course, maneuver, adapt, and evolve. If I am a speedboat in this analogy, then my family is a container ship—enormous and cumbersome, with many contributing parts. We are plodding down the Suez Canal, slow, heavy, and hard to maneuver. It's not that you can't change course in a container ship, but it does take more time and work.

By putting in energy work, over time, you can change how you operate within your family dynamic and how you both perceive and affect your family members—which can lead to a richer family experience, closer relationships, and less trauma. You can start by taking a moment to consider each member of your family and their Dominant Energy: what motivates them, what their priorities are, and the ways they personally derive pleasure. By consciously considering each individual, we can start to experience our family unit in an entirely different light. Maybe we can't transform the ship from a cargo carrier to a speedboat, but we might be able to make a few upgrades to the galley.

NB: Where I refer to the "family" in the following chapters, I am talking about your immediate family. This will likely include your parents and siblings and may include grandparents or any family member who significantly impacts your life. No two families are alike, so please apply the insights in any way you find helpful.

CHAPTER 16

Awakening to Family Energy Patterns

Being around family can have an energy-altering effect on many people. Some deep Dragons become all-feeling, wild, untethered Tigers when they get around their family. Some open Tigers shut down and scale up their Dragon energy as a shield against feeling too much, because staying open can be hard if you don't feel safe (emotionally or otherwise) around your family. It can be frustrating and confusing to be bumped out of our Dominant Energy. If there were ever a time we wanted and needed sure footing, it is when we are amid the chaos of our family dynamic.

If you are like me and you don't see your parents or siblings all that often, they likely won't see the current, evolved version of you when you do get together. It is more likely that your family will see a version of you that they built in their mind through many small and consistent experiences during a time when you were living in close proximity—that is, when you were a kid and teenager.

Given how much you have evolved since your teens, their version of you may be a version that you don't really like or respect; there may even be shame about the person you were yesterday. And while you may be desperate for them to see you as the evolved human you are, interactions can be so brief that it is difficult to provide enough exposure for their perception to substantially change.

Dragons, Stay Grounded

For a Dragon, being perceived by those you love as a person you are not will likely make you feel confined and caged by their view of you—and when a Dragon feels constricted, their instinct is to run and find freedom. And yet what this relationship needs to evolve is for the Dragon to take their Dragon Throne, stand firm in consciousness, and show their family who they are, as best they can, in the limited time they have.

A few years after moving to America, we went back to Australia to spend Christmas with Peter's family. Peter was really looking forward to the reunion. For the first time in years, he finally felt very proud of what he had accomplished: He had moved countries, become an expert in a very complex area of law, set up his own practice, and was now starting to see financial rewards. He had finally developed self-respect and was excited to share his progress and receive recognition from his family, particularly from his successful Dragon father.

From the moment Peter walked through the door on Christmas Day, nothing went to plan. First off, he has a really big family—there are six siblings, and they were all there with their partners and kids—so it was complete chaos. Second, Peter is the youngest of the siblings (he has four older sisters and an older brother), so he sits at the bottom of the established family hierarchy. As usual, everyone was competing for attention and talking over one another, so there was limited time or opportunity for Peter to share his personal and professional evolution. In fact, as he tried to squeeze in his accomplishments, it all came out broken and jumbled, and he was quickly misunderstood, his achievements brushed aside. Needless to say, he felt completely disrespected and diminished.

After a couple of hours, Peter started to deeply crave freedom from everyone. The final straw was when he approached his father to give him a life download, but before he could finish a sentence, his father cut him off and told him that after much thought, he believed Peter should return "home" to Australia and consider rejoining his respected former law firm. Oof. Peter became so upset that after a few heated words with his dad, he stormed off in search of solitude, completely confused by what had just happened. He had been so excited to see everyone. How did it go so wrong?

For one thing, his mom and four older sisters are all wild, chaotic, loving, smothering Tigers. If Peter's family were to have "dominant" energy, it would be Tiger energy. Consequently, the family gatherings are a little chaotic and wild. It's not that the collective family doesn't care about Peter's career; it's that when they get together, they care more about loving him and one another. They get caught up in the pleasure of the reunion and therefore aren't calmly and patiently waiting around to listen to Peter's quarterly business update and feed his Dragon with doses of respect.

The other thing is that Peter's father functions as the family Dragon. Given the very limited time they had together in person, it was clear that Peter's father wanted to use that time to provide Peter with a little wise advice so that Peter could, in his father's opinion, live life to his fullest potential and live at his edge. I'm sure from his perspective, it looked like Peter had given up his career to follow me halfway around the world and was now somewhat lost. True or not, Peter wasn't looking for that advice and direction from his father at Christmastime; he was looking for validation and respect for the immense progress he had made on his current mission. He had turned lemons into lemonade, and he wanted his dad to taste it. But in this instance, Peter's mission was not aligned with his father's mission, and the end result was frustration and a feeling of having been disrespected.

When Peter was able to take a step back and view his family through the Dragon-Tiger energy lens, he could see the complex family dynamics that had played out and triggered his reaction.

If you recall from Part II, "a Dragon will find real freedom when they can learn to escape the pain of their ego, self-doubt, and judgment."

Peter was feeling a wave of pain triggered by his ego. But by rising above that pain, Peter could clearly see that there was no master plot being carried out by his family to disrespect him; everyone had the best intentions. There was freedom for Peter in that knowledge.

Now when Peter catches up with his family, instead of being drawn into the chaos, he can step back and marvel at it, even appreciate it. He watches his mother and sisters' beautiful, wild hurricane from the outside, without getting drawn into their storm or upset by it. Instead of waiting to update his dad during the chaotic Tiger-family dynamic, he now calls him regularly. Away from the full-family intensity, Peter takes the time to walk his father through his complex business, his vision, his mission, and the progress he has made on his journey. And after fully understanding it, his father gives Peter the respect and validation he is looking for.

In order to enjoy his family gatherings, Peter needed to stay grounded, present, and strong. He had to go deep and take the Dragon Throne, rather than follow his impulse to retreat to his den of solitude. If you cannot stand firm, you will never get the chance to show your family the Dragon you truly are. And as we have established by now, you're a badass.

Tigers, Stay Open

While being misperceived by family makes a Dragon feel disrespected, for a Tiger, being misperceived is a soul-destroying violation of their deep desire to be truly seen and loved by those who matter most. If anyone should truly see me, know me, and love me, it should be my family—right?

In order to be seen, however, we Tigers need to be truly open and show ourselves. I have learned to bring my dominant Tiger energy to almost every area of my life, but the hardest place for me to open up has been with my family. I have found that when I get around my family, I continually close up and go into Dragon mode. I avoid my feelings when I am around them; I pull back from emotional conversations and find it hard to let go into my pleasure when they are around. I couldn't tell you the last time I laughed with my family. Instead, I find myself "doing stuff": driving them around, cooking, cleaning, and just being busy.

But being in my Dragon around my family isn't deeply fulfilling or sustainable. I am not showing them my authentic self, which means that I don't feel deeply seen or deeply loved. That love can only flow if I allow myself to open up, show them my heart, and receive their love.

The issue is that staying open can be hard if you don't feel safe (physically, emotionally . . . whatever that word means to you). As we learned in Part IV, to really let go and feel their pleasure, Tigers need to feel safe. And for me it felt as if every time I would relax and let go, that was when our family interactions were the worst.

What I needed to recognize is that I'm an adult now, and I can keep myself safe.

Once I finally became confident in my own safety, I was free to open up and stay in my Tiger energy around my family more easily, with less fear. If my dad decides to snap and carry on like an asshole, he is free to do that in the same way I am free to get in my car and go home or hang up the phone. However, closing my heart to avoid being hurt won't stop him from having his moments, and it won't stop me from being hurt in those moments, but it will stop me from experiencing pleasure in the positive moments and the joy of a deep connection where I feel seen and loved.

When I started to maintain confidence in my safety and to open my heart with my family, everything changed. I am now blown away by my parents commenting that "I look and sound so happy" and by how much joy seeing that brings them. We now connect at a deeper level, and I can spend more time with them in my Tiger energy without feeling drained by my Dragon defenses.

We all have our own family challenges. I encourage you to take a moment to reflect on your family dynamic. How do you feel when you're around your immediate family?

If the interactions are triggering for you, then take some time to contemplate whether adjusting your energy could assist. Using energy consciousness in conjunction with other therapy work can provide deep healing and help lead you closer to your pleasure. After all, families are made up of many, many different members and permutations (parents, siblings, cousins, grandparents, sons/daughters/progeny, step-everything, etc.) and each member impacts us in their own way.

Without taking away from the impacts of those relationships on our lives, I will be focusing on our relationships with our parents (as opposed to, say, you as a parent of your children) in the following two chapters. The reason is that for the majority of us, our relationships with our parents have the greatest impact on our lives and our energy. We came from them, our energy flows from their energy, they are deeply invested in us, and we stay connected in some manner or another throughout our entire lives. That said, a lot of these insights will be applicable to other family relationships and may also help you with your own parenting approach.

Your Dragon Parent

We know from Part II that Dragons spend their life chasing their freedom, focused on their purpose and missions. Believe it or not, this also applies to your Dragon parent. Like all Dragons, your Dragon parent moves through their life from one mission to the next, with each mission feeling more important than the last as they grow, evolve, and deepen their consciousness.

For many Dragons, they feel the deepest and most motivating purpose they have ever felt the moment their first child is born. After looking into their baby's eyes, all other missions dissolve. Those missions suddenly seem miniscule and frivolous compared to the gigantic mission before them. This mission is usually some version of the following:

"I must do everything in my power to ensure that my child has every opportunity to live their fullest life and realize their greatest potential."

This translates differently for each Dragon. For some it could mean devoting their time and attention to monitoring and mentoring; for others it might mean working harder and longer to ensure they provide financial security. No matter the approach, from the moment their child can walk and talk, a devoted Dragon parent will encourage and coach that child (in the best way they know how) to walk down a path that nurtures the child's talents, skills, and abilities in an attempt to produce the best possible successor.

Based on their informed adult opinion and through the lens of their own experiences, your Dragon parent will also start to form a view (consciously or subconsciously) of what you, their child, is *capable of*, and they will make it their mission to try to get you to *live up to that potential.*

Here's where the conflict begins, particularly if you are a Dragon child.

Dragon Child of a Dragon Parent

If you are a Dragon child, most of your life is centered on finding your edge and obtaining your freedom. When it comes to finding your edge, you are on a mission to determine *what you are capable of*—what universal rules apply to you. Can you fly? Are you strong? Are you the "fastest" kid in your class? The "smartest"?

At the same time, your Dragon parent is also forming a view of what you are capable of. Your Dragon parent may have "decided" your potential before you have even had a chance to test your own limits. So for Dragon kids, the search for your edge of potential can easily get derailed and diverted into an effort to find freedom from your Dragon parent's control, expectations, and criticism—another form of phantom freedom.

You believe that you will be happy when you are free from your Dragon parent's expectations, because those expectations look like a predetermined path for your future, chosen by someone who may not actually know you as well as they think they know you. And a predetermined path does not look or feel like freedom. It feels like another dungeon that must be escaped.

Ironically, once you break free of that predetermined expectation and are in control of your purpose and destiny, you will find yourself drawn back to the dungeon to seek and obtain your Dragon parent's approval and respect for your chosen path. Your mission thereby becomes circular: You want to be free to choose your own path, but once you have chosen it, you want to be validated and respected for your choices.

As I mentioned in the previous chapter, Peter was the baby of six children, which resulted in him being mollycoddled by his four older sisters, as well as his parents. That dynamic was exacerbated by the fact that he had a very complicated birth where both he and his mom almost died, and then as he grew he suffered from adolescent epilepsy. From Peter's perspective, it felt as if his father treated him differently from the rest of his siblings; he was just so happy that his son was alive and healthy. To Peter that translated into the feeling that his Dragon-dad maintained extremely low expectations for him.

Notwithstanding these perceived low expectations (and probably in part because of them), Peter performed well at school and got higher scores than any of his older siblings, who all did very well in their own right. When he was accepted to law school, his dad (who is also a lawyer) simply encouraged him to "get through." Basically, to Peter it felt as if his father maintained low expectations for him every step of the way, and then when Peter would exceed his expectations, he would merely say things like, "Don't get ahead of yourself."

As Peter grew and evolved, it felt to him as if his father stayed rigid in his view of what Peter's life would be and what he could achieve. It was only after the birth of our second daughter—also a time when Peter's career really started to explode—that his father finally acknowledged Peter's achievements. It was a beautiful inter- action to watch unfold. And yet the acknowledgment wasn't exactly what Peter had expected. While his father gave Peter the validation he sought, he also became very introspective about his own career and started to share with Peter his own contemplation as to whether he could have pushed his own potential further.

Gaining respect from a Dragon parent can be a double-edged sword. When you fall short of your Dragon parent's expectations for you, you will likely feel their disapproval. Alternatively, if you exceed their expectations, while they will certainly be proud of you and respect you, they may also feel uncomfortable pangs of jealousy. After all, Dragons are naturally competitive, and you being their progeny can't change that. Still, you should not pull back from your potential to please a Dragon parent any more than you should try to live beyond your potential to please them.

To this day, anytime Peter experiences a success in his life, the first person he will call is his father. Gaining his father's ongoing respect and approval is still important for him; that desire will never really end. But Peter no longer allows his father's approval or dis- appointment to influence his mission or purpose. Now that he has forged his own path and received respect for those choices, he feels free to live out his own existence.

As hard as it can be, try not to let your Dragon parent's expec- tations shackle you. Letting their high (or low) expectations direct your journey is like letting the tail wag the dog (or should I say the Dragon). Instead, find your own purpose and find your own edge.

The irony is that your Dragon parent will respect you for living your own life to your fullest potential. They will respect you for finding your edge of potential, because that was ultimately their life mission all along.

Tiger Child of a Dragon Parent

If you are the Tiger child, your relationship with your Dragon parent will have its own unique challenges. Where a Dragon child will try to escape the expectations of a Dragon parent and their watchful eye, a Tiger child is jumping up and down waving their arms screaming, "Look at me, look at me!"

My mom is a Tiger, and my dad is a very dominant Dragon. I always knew that I had my mother's love—she was wonderfully attentive, nurturing, and loving—but I felt as if I had to work hard to get my father's attention. He and my brother would spend hours and hours on projects together. They would spend the weekends building go-karts, training for triathlons, honing their rugby skills, and preparing crab pots. I can now see that these were all little missions that gave my brother and my father a deep sense of purpose, achievement, and self-respect.

Yet as Tiger children, we don't have the cognitive maturity to comprehend the "purpose-driven" Dragon parent. (Hell, even as Tiger adults, understanding this is hard.) The deeper your parent is in their Dragon energy, the harder it will be to break through. The Tiger will wonder, "How can they care more about their purpose than feeling and giving their Tiger child love?" And sometimes it will feel impossible to capture and maintain their attention, which can make you feel unseen and unloved.

I speak to my mom most days but will probably only talk to my dad once a week or every other week. And after some initial banter about the weather or the state of the world, he will steer the conversation toward his business. Every. Single. Time. Even after I left the family business, he still wanted to talk shop with me whenever he could. As a Tiger, I felt as if his purpose and I were eternally in a competition for his affection. I finally said to him, "I can't wait until you sell your business so we can go back to having normal conversations that don't involve work." The look on his face conveyed complete confusion.

I know now that talking about his business with me is not "work" for him. It is him sharing his life's work and his ultimate purpose—it is a way to obtain my respect. By telling him I didn't want to talk about it, I was disrespecting him in the deepest way imaginable.

Now that I understand why my dad is always talking about work—that is, now that I know it is not because he loves his work more than me, but that his work is his world—I have more tolerance for the conversation. I've also found that love and attention flow more easily and freely when I dish out doses of respect to him on a regular basis. Similar to Peter, when I dish out respect, he reciprocates with his time and attention.

Also like Peter, my dad really just wants to see me happy. While the Dragon parent wants their Dragon child to reach their potential, the Dragon parent also wants to see their Tiger child *safe and happy*. Don't get me wrong: Your Dragon parent also wants you to excel in life, but what they want most of all is to see that your heart is taken care of and filled with pleasure.

The only time I have heard my dad cry was when I told him about Peter's infidelity. He was shattered. We wept together over the phone. After the dust had settled, he flew from Australia to the United States to make sure I was okay and the kids were okay. What surprised me was that, despite how angry he was with Peter, he was able to forgive Peter when it was clear we were going to try to work it out. Ultimately, my dad wants me to be safe and happy, and if I felt safe and happy staying with Peter, then he did not want to stand in the way.

The biggest gift I can give to my dad is to open my Tiger heart and show him that I am happy. And I am, so I make sure he knows it.

Dealing with a Dragon Parent

No matter whether you yourself are a Dragon or a Tiger, if you have a Dragon parent, keep in mind that you are one of their missions—an important mission, but just one of many that your Dragon parent will have in their lives. And aren't we all just living our own life? Your job will be to stay centered in your own energy. If you are a Dragon, too, try to empathize with your parent's missions without letting their expectations shape your own path. If you are a Tiger, do not expect them to share their feelings with you or even join you in your own feelings and emotions. But don't let that stop you from sharing with them.

CHAPTER 18

Your Tiger Parent

Now let's talk about your Tiger parent—that open, loving, nurturing, forgiving, emotionally enduring heart and soul of the family.

For most children, their relationship with their Tiger parent is pretty special. Tiger parents can help quench their Tiger child's deep desire to be truly seen and loved, dispensing an infinite supply of attention and devotion. And for the Dragon child, the Tiger parent provides them with encouragement and support to go into the world and realize their purpose and potential, while also fortifying a safehold where the Dragon can return to recharge and replenish before breaking free once more.

That all sounds amazing, doesn't it?

While our Tiger parents are very special, we also know that they aren't without their flaws. Tiger parents tend to have a deep sense of longing for "more" from their children: more affection, more closeness, more time! After all, while our Tiger parents are *parents*, they are also just *Tigers*—those wild, untethered, all-loving, all-feeling nurturers on an endless quest to fill up with pleasure. And what is more pleasurable than giving and receiving love and affection from a child? For some, this is a great thing, while for others (like me) this is an ongoing challenge that can cause tension and conflict for both Tiger and Dragon children alike.

Dragon Child of a Tiger Parent

Dragons, no one softens that scaly exterior of yours like your Tiger parent. Who doesn't enjoy a relationship where you are loved unconditionally and the subject of deep devotion?

But nothing is perfect, and there are two areas in particular where your Tiger parent's desire for more of you can easily result in tussle and tension. The first is when it comes to resolving conflict, and the second is when you enter into a committed relationship.

Let's start with the conflict. When dissension surfaces between you and your Tiger parent, you likely do what Dragons do best: You become evasive, withdraw, and seek solitude. Unfortunately for you, the further you withdraw and the more you resist the topic of tension, the more your Tiger parent will attempt to "storm" the issue. They're a Tiger, and as we covered in Chapter 10, your Tiger parent wants to maximize the issue to the same extent that your inner Dragon wants to minimize it.

It was always hard to watch my Tiger mom and Dragon brother argue. The disagreement would begin with the current issue at hand—say, about my brother not getting a good grade—and then, when he would evade the argument or try to use humor to laugh it off, Mom would immediately mistake his use of humor for indifference. Of course he cared. Of course he was sad about his C in English—he was dealing with his own doubt and shame around being a failure and feeling stupid. But because he was dealing with it privately, silently, she would misinterpret that as contempt for his education and therefore his future. As a result, her frustration escalated.

The issue then went from the bad grade to him not appreciating the opportunities she worked hard to give him, to the reckless driving last Thursday, to the broken curfew two weeks ago, to the girlfriend she didn't like. . . . The complaint would get bigger and bigger as she attempted to draw him out and engage. But all this would do was make him emotionally and physically disengage even further. He would simply leave.

In the interest of conflict resolution (as hard as it is for you to do), resist the temptation to pull away and evade the issue at hand but rather stand firm and take the Dragon Throne so that the conflict can be given a chance to de-escalate. And if you can convince your Tiger parent to limit the conversation to the immediate issue at hand, the two of you might just be able to resolve things. But don't worry: If the issue doesn't get resolved today, your Tiger parent has a wonderful memory and will be sure to resurface the exact same issue at another time when you least expect it. (Do I speak from experience? Why yes, I do.) So try to resolve the issue today to stop it from coming back tomorrow.

Another common and interesting challenge can arise when you choose a partner, particularly if that partner looks to become your committed life partner. When you finally give your commitment to a partner, your Tiger parent may feel as if there is less love and space for them in your life, which in some ways is true. Dragons are purpose- and mission-focused, so when you pop your head up from your current mission and look around to dish out a little consciousness and love, the person closest to you—your partner—will receive the lion's share (or Tiger's share, I should say). Your Tiger parent knows this and will feel your absence deeply.

You shouldn't avoid relationships or feel shame or guilt about this energy shift, but it does help you to understand your Tiger parent's perspective. If they start to act "irrationally" or whip up a Tiger storm, you can see that they might be having an emotional reaction to you entering a new life stage. It can also explain why your Tiger parent, who is usually so supportive of everything you do, is being uncharacteristically harsh to your new love interest.

Remember, your Tiger parent has devoted their life to loving you and anticipating and fulfilling your needs. And deep down, your Tiger parent knows you need to leave the den and find a life mate, so they want to ensure that their "replacement" is going to devote themselves as completely to you as they have. They want to see that you have found a partner who will love you deeply, surrender to your awesomeness, and take care of your heart. They don't want to part with their baby Dragon unless they feel certain that you will be taken care of, body and soul.

These noble intentions can cause real conflict, because you will likely choose a partner who best supports your life purpose (whatever that is at the time), whereas your Tiger parent wants you to choose a partner who will support your heart—which is not always the same person. Ultimately, however, that choice is a freedom reserved for you. And as much as that might frustrate your Tiger parent, they need to suck it up and learn to appreciate your partner for their role in supporting you in achieving your purpose and freedom.

In the end, you know that your Tiger parent will love you no matter what—whether you walk away from an argument, fail in your career, miss out on life goals, or choose the "wrong" partner. The love and devotion of a Tiger is a constant you can return to when you need to let down your guard, lick your wounds, and take a breath before going back out into your purpose-driven Dragon world.

Tiger Child of a Tiger Parent

I always felt as if my mom wanted more from me than I was able to give. We could spend all weekend together, work in the same office, have dinner, sleep under the same roof, and I am sure she would still say, "We don't get any time together!"

What I now understand (particularly as a mother myself who wants "more" from my own daughters) is that she is a Tiger, just like me, with an unquenchable thirst to be seen and loved. However, unlike me (although like many women of her generation), she only has a very small community to turn to for the love that she needs. My dad, like so many stoic Australian men of his generation, was fairly withholding with his affection, and he was also constantly off on any number of Dragon missions.

Therefore, when I was open and in my receiving Tiger energy, she would feel that and start to really let go, rupture, and unload her feelings onto me—as Tigers do. This used to freak me out. I didn't want to see my mom rupture! Watching her rupture would push me into my Dragon energy, where I would either run away from her or stay and try to fix everything for her. What I now realize is that she didn't need that from me; she already had enough Dragons in her life. What she needed was my Tiger. Every time I clenched my open Tiger heart in a Dragon fist, I was blocking our ability to go deeper into love and our connection.

Still, as a Tiger, it can be hard to weather a Tiger parent's storm on your own, particularly if that parent is angry or upset and directing the power of their storm in your direction. If, like me, you are surrounded by a family of Dragons, when the storm erupts and the Dragons take flight, you may be the only one left in the room, so it will *feel* as if your Tiger parent is "taking it all out on you." If they aren't being careful and conscientious, they probably are. After all, you are there, and they need to feel things through.

Well, Tigers, remember that this works both ways. How many times have you stormed at your Tiger parent because they happened to be the one in the room? I can't begin to count the number of times I have done that to my poor mom.

The good news is that by weathering each other's storms, you help fortify your relationship. But it can be a lot—too much, sometimes. That's why it's necessary to establish some boundaries with your Tiger parent. This can be as simple as a mental boundary where you know "it's not all about you."

When your Tiger parent starts to storm, try asking them, "What is this *really* about?" or, "How does that make you feel?" Try to get to the bottom of the emotions that are driving the storm. You may have contributed to the storm, but you probably didn't create the entire thing. So try to move your Tiger parent from their head to their heart to help to diffuse the situation. As you know, empathy goes a long way during a Tiger storm.

Now that I have more empathy for my mom, I find it much easier to relax into my own Tiger when we are together, and we have a much better, more authentic connection. Mom and I are never better than when I embrace her love and attention and allow her to truly nurture me. She immediately flew to my side and listened to me cry for months when I was dealing with Peter's infidelity, and she helped me sleep and heal after each daughter was born, as well as after my plastic surgeries. In a strange energetic shift, when I allow her to truly care for me and love me without all of my Dragon defenses getting in the way, that is when we are the closest. And I imagine I'll find that when I can do the same for her, we will grow even closer.

Dealing with a Tiger Parent

Dragons and Tigers alike relish the love and support that Tiger parents shower on us—at least up to a point. The challenge is usually establishing boundaries, especially as we near and enter adulthood, so that we can live our own lives even as our Tiger parent wants more from us. Navigating those boundaries can be tricky for us all, though in different ways depending on our own Dominant Energy. The trick is to not let our Tiger parent push us away from our Dominant Energy as we react to what can seem to be an emotional onslaught. Stay grounded.

Improving Family Dynamics

When it comes to improving family dynamics, as with most things, consciousness is key. Try to take a step back and consider the energy of your family members. Which are dominant Dragons and which are dominant Tigers? How do they make you feel when you are around one another? Perhaps you go deeper into your dominance, or perhaps they bump you out of your comfort zone. Try to pay attention to how your energy shifts in their presence.

Just by understanding that your Tiger family members are looking to be seen and loved and to find their pleasure, you can get the most out of your time with them without feeling frustrated when certain expectations aren't met. Similarly, knowing that a sibling or a parent is a dominant Dragon can allow you to improve the relationship by feeding them respect.

By giving your family members doses of what they need, you will find that they will be more attuned to feeding you what you need. And if they aren't, stay conscious enough to let the triggers pass you like ships in the night. Because even if you don't get the love or respect from your family that you were craving, you will at least love and respect yourself for staying present and grounded throughout your time with them.

Here are a few takeaways to help you improve those family dynamics:

DRAGONS

1. Stand firm in consciousness and show your family who you are, as best you can, in the limited time you have.

2. Try not to let your Dragon parent's expectations shackle you. Letting their high (or low) expectations direct your journey is like letting the tail wag the dog (or should I say the Dragon). Instead find your own purpose and find your own edge.

3. When resolving a dispute with your Tiger parent, resist the temptation to pull away and evade the issue at hand. Rather, stand firm and take the Dragon Throne so the conflict can be given a chance to de-escalate.

4. Try not to allow your Tiger parent to influence your relationship choices. Choose the partner who supports your purpose and enjoy the freedom that relationship brings.

TIGERS

1. Staying open can be hard if you don't feel safe (no matter what that word means to you). Know that as an adult, you can keep yourself safe. Feel your own safety and open your heart so that you can shower your family with your love and light, and thereby stay open to receiving their love in return.

2. Try not to let your Dragon parent's mission-centric focus make you feel unseen and unloved. Instead, feed your Dragon parent with respect and watch as they reciprocate with their time and attention.

3. Show your Dragon parent when you are safe and happy.

4. When your Tiger parent starts to storm, try to move them from their head into their heart. Try to determine the feelings behind their words.

PART VII

Workplace Energy

From a young age we all receive Dragon training in how to "do": how to stay focused, meet deadlines, follow instructions, and deliver results. By the time we start our careers, we feel fairly prepared to work . . . like Dragons.

Yet business and cultural changes have shown that in order to achieve sustainable success, we need a balance of Dragon and Tiger energy. Today's businesses are no longer just about profit and traditional output measures. Instead, success is now characterized by innovation, flexibility, intuition, and a people-oriented approach— all of which are much more ethereal, Tiger-centric abilities. Striking an *energetic balance* is critical if we are going to unlock our potential.

Why? Because the ultimate purpose of business is profit, right? That's what makes it a business. And while most businesses are also trying to innovate and help people or the planet in some way, many have investors who, at some point in time, want to receive a return on their investment. Yet without great people performing at their best, it is nearly impossible to scale anything, and that includes profits. And without profits, it is nearly impossible to recruit and retain good people . . . so the dance continues between Dragon and Tiger energy.

Energetic balance isn't something we've spent a lot of time considering in this book, because in our primary relationship we have been focused on creating an energetic *imbalance*—that is, leaning into our Dominant Energy to create sexual tension in our relationship. And yet at work we need to strive for a slightly different and more well-rounded approach.

I'm not saying you should stop being a Tiger or stop being a Dragon—staying in your Dominant Energy is still best to ensure you feel that you are being authentic—but I am saying to be mindful of your dominant strengths and shortcomings. Leaning into both your Tiger and your Dragon can assist you in reaching your greatest potential in the workplace.

In the next chapter, I'll use my own business history to illustrate how the Dragon and Tiger approaches to work can either come together to create a more resilient workplace or clash to create chaos. Subsequent chapters take a closer look at first Dragons and then Tigers and tips to help them thrive in the workplace.

As we move through these chapters, don't lose sight of the fact that the bedroom and the boardroom are different places; therefore, it should be no surprise that they require different energetic approaches.

CHAPTER 19

Dragons and Tigers in the Same Cage

Several years ago, I was hired as the head of sales for an Inc. 500 US company to boost revenue after they had a year of stagnation. This was a perfect Dragon challenge. I had purpose-in-a-box.

I started where any self-respecting Dragon would start . . . with the numbers. I labored over our lead funnels, our cost per lead, and our close rates. I completed countless missions: updating our sales tools, processes, and systems. But none of that moved the needle. I struggled to gain traction.

After ninety days, sales were still stagnant, but then a gift fell into my lap, or should I say, a sales coach and mentor by the name of Lisa McLeod. Lisa is the author of the 2012 book *Selling with Noble Purpose.*

The research behind Lisa's strategy proved that sales teams who sell with a "noble purpose"—who truly want to make a difference to their customers or the planet—outsell transactional sellers who focus on targets and quotas. Organizations with a purpose bigger than money outperform their competition by over 350 percent. And a culture of purpose and meaning is the single-biggest factor for attracting and retaining great people.

After reading her book, we decided to hire Lisa to speak at our conference and to work with our sales team to develop our noble purpose. We then changed the way we spoke internally, as well as the way we engaged with our customers, stakeholders, and vendors. We put improving the lives of our customers front and center. We opened our sales meetings with stories of how we had changed lives, and we read letters from our customers to one another before we looked at our metrics. We started to have more heart, and that turned into more fun. We found a way to work together, play together, and really perform. Our commitment to our profits was now aligned with our commitment to our people. We found the perfect Tiger/Dragon balance and the sales started flowing . . . fast. We went from roughly $15 million to $30 million in revenue in 18 months.

Dragon Focus, Tiger Chaos

We loved our long days and lived for our after-work drinks, during which we shared war stories till 2 a.m. Our team became close, like family, and we had trust and momentum holding us together. We were growing fast, and while we were stressed, we were happy.

Then cracks started to emerge. We felt as though the team that had successfully delivered us from stagnation to rapid sales growth did not necessarily have the skills or sophistication to get us to the next level of performance. So we made the decision to go on a massive recruitment drive and hire a lot of new, shiny, smart, and—ultimately—expensive people. While the business was doing great, we still had payroll ratios to maintain, so as much as we would have loved to keep everyone, we also made the hard decisions to let some people go. And in my infinite Dragon wisdom, I decided to do that the week before Christmas. My thinking was logically sound—let people go on December 22 and then start my new shiny motivated team on January 2. We would hit the ground running for the new year!

What I got was a fucking mess.

The team members who remained were sad and disappointed that their friends and colleagues had been let go. They thought it was cruel doing it the week before Christmas. They resented the new employees—whom they viewed as the "replacements" for the team they had known and trusted—and certainly did not make them feel welcome. It was "us" and "them." The new crew felt the palpable tension and started to question what sort of toxic culture they had just joined. And despite reassuring everyone that we were not making any further redundancies, the damage was done. We were in a state of chaos.

Tigers find their happiness through pleasure, and in order to find their pleasure they need to feel safe (as we covered in Chapter 8). Our Tigers no longer felt safe, and they were certainly not happy. So the Tigers stopped *acting* and started *reacting*. The fearful Tiger energy began to overwhelm the office, causing so much chaos that it became impossible to manage everyone. People started arriving late, leaving early, taking long lunches, playing Uno in the lunchroom at 3 p.m. . . . basically anything other than work. The Tiger energy at the office became so dominant that even some deep Dragons got pulled in and joined the chaos.

Meanwhile, the remainder of the Dragons who stayed in their dominant Dragon energy did in fact become motivated by the pressure; they loved seeing the numbers, so they put their heads down and got after the task at hand. We loved these Dragons and wanted the entire office to respond the same way, with the thrill of fear helping them to perform at their best. Those Dragons could see the gains to be made amid the volatility. There were jobs to fill, promotions to step into, and plenty of opportunities to demonstrate their commitment and worth.

Our Dragons did their best to avoid the drama of the Tigers. But no matter how hard the deep Dragons worked, the Tiger chaos cut them off at their knees. It was only a matter of time before some of the motivated Dragons jumped ship to find a less chaotic workplace. I recall one of our top-performing Dragons commenting during an exit interview that our office "had more clowns than a circus." The office really had started to feel carnivalesque.

We eventually stabilized the culture by going back to basics. By releasing some of the performance pressure, making a few leadership changes, bringing back some warm familiar faces, and, ultimately, staying true to our noble purpose. We went back to focusing on the importance of our customers and helping improve their lives above all else. It took a year, but the carnival was over. The business today is thriving, the culture is balanced, and they continue to experience exceptional growth.

It was a wild year, a steep learning curve, and a fascinating case study of energy forces in the workplace.

A Delicate Balance

At the time, of course, I didn't have the clear mental framework or vocabulary that I have now to understand or explain the way that Dragon and Tiger energies were creating destructive patterns in the workplace. I didn't know I was allowing my Dragon energy to take over or that by failing to create a safe place for feelings, I was letting down my fellow Tigers.

Now I can appreciate that creating a balance of pressure and pleasure where everyone on our team could thrive is the key to generating profits. Creating this balance is not easy, but it is important. To truly succeed in the long term, businesses need to strike a delicate balance between profits and people.

Learning to see and understand the differences between Dragons and Tigers is the first step to creating balance. And what I observed is that, as with our relationships, where we saw triggers and recurring challenges like stress, money, and sex, there are a few hot spots that shine a light on the different energetic motivators in Dragons vs. Tigers in the workplace. These are how we view *profits and people*, how we respond to *pressure and pleasure*, and how we approach *negotiations*. With those focus areas in mind, let me take you on a deeper dive into how Dragons and Tigers can thrive or fail in the workplace.

CHAPTER 20

Dragons at Work

It is no surprise that Dragon energy has historically dominated the workplace. Dragons are motivated by purpose, and a career is purpose-in-a-box. Dragon energy also thrives on stress, competition, accomplishment, and respect, and the workplace delivers these motivators in spades. But the workplace is all about balance, not Polarity, and achieving the Dragon missions requires just a touch of Tiger.

Pay Attention to People, Not Just Profits

Profits are a measure that Dragons understand. As discussed in Chapter 14, Dragons are competitive by nature, and money allows them to objectively measure success and, whether right or wrong, even their worth. Yet, if a Dragon completely ignores the people, culture, ethics, and values of a business—even if they are a highly profitable contributor to the business—most companies will still

fire them. Thus over time, successful Dragons have learned, sometimes the hard way, that they can't be all about the money.

That said, if you're a Dragon in a solo career where your actions
only directly impact yourself, then perhaps you don't need to worry
about those pesky people standing in your way. But if your career
requires you to leverage the skills of others or demands that you collaborate with a team, then you will need to temper that mono-focus
in order to truly excel, because times really have changed.

So, Dragons, when it comes to your career, finding the balance
between achieving your purpose and caring for people is absolutely
critical. That includes your team members, vendors, customers, and
the community at large. To get the most out of everyone, we need
to engage their hearts, as well as their pockets.

As a Dragon leader, you must try to be less transactional and
more open in your dialogue. This means putting in effort to
understand and appreciate your team, their motivations, and their
priorities. Gathering those insights will take time, and sometimes
that means time away from what a Dragon needs to "do." Yet the
time is well spent, because the end result is that your team will feel
more engaged and will perform better overall. Plus, you can actually spend less time "doing" and more time mentoring if you are
surrounded by great people. As a Dragon, you will simply need to
reframe your purpose from one of self-interest to one of mentor-
ship where the mission is now for everyone to be exceptional, not
just you.

When you do find yourself deep in your Dragon energy—
and inevitably feeling frustrated with all the people slowing you
down—instead of burning it all to the ground, take a step back,
seek out a little solitude, and try to see the big picture. It might feel
counterintuitive to step back when you want to charge forward, but
your career or business is not a timed sport; there is no whistle that
blows to declare a winner. Your career lasts a lifetime. Try to relax

into your Tiger a little and connect with those around you. Have a laugh, join the work lunch, or take a walk to grab a coffee. The work will be there waiting for you, I promise.

Adding a Little Tiger to My Dragon Energy

Early on in my career, my Dragon energy led me to accidentally create a culture where my team felt as if they were always bothering me, that I wasn't overly approachable as opposed to them feeling mentored and supported. Even as my career evolved and I transitioned from being an individual sales director to running sales teams—still strongly in my Dragon energy—I initially found myself feeling frustrated by the time it took to manage and mentor my crew. I felt as if there was always someone walking into my office, interrupting me with a question or a problem. I thought, "How in the world will I ever get my work done if I am constantly interrupted?"

Over time, however, I realized that as a leader, I needed to learn to find a better balance between my Dragon and Tiger energies and embrace a little more of my Tiger so I could be more flexible and fluid. I could no longer arrive at work and check tasks off my to-do list. I needed to be available for my team to help problem-solve so they could be as productive as possible. As a leader I could no longer be a 100 percent task-focused Dragon; I would need to lean into my fluid, flexible, supportive Tiger. I needed to learn how to delegate (something that doesn't come easily to Dragons who are used to doing everything themselves!). I needed to serve in order to lead. I needed to let go. When I finally made that change, I saw a dramatic difference in both the productivity and camaraderie of my team.

Dragons Find Pleasure in Pressure

Dragons love pressure. Pressure to perform allows a Dragon to test their abilities and find their edge of potential in the moment. A deadline also means that a Dragon can justify working around the clock to achieve their mission, with little to no distractions. A stressful deadline allows a Dragon to silence competing priorities for a moment in time and simply work on their project, which is what they really want to do (but aren't usually allowed to do because of other things demanding their time and attention). This is a relief and can actually feel like a form of freedom, because Dragon energy is not great at multitasking in the first place. By having an excuse to be singularly focused, the Dragon can feel strong and confident instead of feeling as though they are trying (and failing) to juggle their work alongside all the other elements of their life.

When (and if) your workplace is pressure-fueled, pay attention to the energy of your coworkers, and try to avoid being pulled into the emotional drama. I've seen many strong Dragons get lured into the Tiger chaos. Stay on mission, go deep into your Dragon, and remember your purpose.

Alternatively, if your workplace is the opposite and there isn't a great deal of pressure, you might find yourself feeling bored, restless, and unmotivated. In that environment you may need to create a sense of internal pressure to push yourself to your edge. It will be important to set your own personal goals and deadlines. When I worked in a slow, relaxed, bureaucratic environment, I personally spent money and hired my own accountability coach to help me to advance my career and objectives. I paid a coach to apply the pressure my workplace failed to provide.

If you are a Dragon leader, be conscious of the collective energy environment you and your leadership team are creating. I've seen Dragon leaders try to exclusively hire and retain deep Dragons.

They set about creating a high-pressure-driven, dominant-Dragon culture. I assure you, however, that such an experiment is destined to fail because it creates a very imbalanced workplace. Filling a workplace with deeply dominant Dragons and excessive pressure can generate other challenges, like hyper-aggression and toxic competitiveness. In those environments, it is the client or customer who usually suffers the most as competitive Dragons cut corners to win.

Finding a balance is key, as is taking an individual approach to performance and motivation. What applies to your Dragon employees may not work for your Tiger employees. You can't avoid pressure and deadlines—in fact you shouldn't!—but sometimes you need to take your foot off the pedal knowing that your Tigers don't do their best work under constant pressure.

If you want to get the most out of your Tiger team, showing appreciation and encouraging their need for pleasure from time to time will actually help productivity. Tigers also struggle to do their best work in an environment where they feel unsafe, so creating a stable environment where your team—particularly the more conservative Tigers—can have a voice and share their concerns will help improve overall satisfaction and performance.

How Dragons Can Improve Negotiations

Whether it's a deal, a promotion, or a pay rise, the art of negotiation is a recurring skill that we need throughout our careers. This is another area where, at least on the surface, Dragon energy excels. Negotiating is a form of challenge, and Dragons love a good challenge.

When a Dragon is negotiating, they have a clear mission: to push their agenda forward and get the best result for themselves, their team, or their business. If the Dragon can come back to the office having negotiated a successful deal for their company or arrive home after negotiating a pay rise, they feel like a knight riding back from conquest to a parade of roses. They can smell the respect in the air.

So yes, negotiating is an exceptional Dragon skill. But as you can probably predict, balance is key. Dragons tend to put their purpose over people, which means that if relationships break down but the deal gets done, all in all, they're pretty happy. And if the Dragon needs to walk away and alienate people because the deal isn't good enough, they'll do that too. Dragons will take the respect they receive from walking away over the disrespect of negotiating a bad deal.

If that sounds like you, then try to be cognizant of the people on the other side of the negotiation. Try to maintain a pathway back to good relations if you can. If you are a Dragon leader responsible for negotiating promotions and pay rises, it is important to understand that not everyone enjoys negotiating as much as you. Not everyone will stand up for their worth. Your exceptional Tiger team members are likely to leave rather than fight with you over their value, because a Tiger doesn't enjoy having to justify their worth to you. Watch your rock star Tigers as closely as you watch your rock star Dragons, and make sure you are compensating them equally. Just because a Tiger didn't go hard negotiating for what they are worth doesn't mean they shouldn't be looked after and respected.

And if you can't financially compensate them, know that money isn't everything to a Tiger. A title change, a better office, public recognition, or a deep and detailed feedback session where you acknowledge their achievements might all be equally as rewarding to your Tiger team.

Your Dragon employees, on the other hand, will generally have no issues asking for a promotion or negotiating their own compensation. A Dragon is more likely to simply consider their potential and ask for what they want, because they are less concerned with rejection than they are with reaching their potential. This is the same logic the Dragon follows when they apply for jobs: Even if they aren't qualified, they still go for what they want. So watch for the underqualified Dragon—they may be the most aggressive and assertive team member, but they may not be the most qualified. Don't overlook talented Tigers just because they may be more reserved.

Shed a Little Dragon Skin

You Dragons out there probably already know that you are highly valued in the workplace, because traditional practices recognize and reward people who get things done. And there may be some jobs where the laser focus of a Dragon on a mission is all that an organization needs from you. But most jobs—frontline to leadership—in companies today require Dragons to allow a little of their inner Tiger to shine through. You don't need to throw off your Dragon skin entirely. Instead, create space to think about the people you work with, as well as the profits you want to make, and remember that not everyone will thrive under pressure like you do.

CHAPTER 21

Tigers at Work

After my family trauma in my early twenties pushed me into my Dragon, I found a refuge in the workplace. I could eat and breathe my work, and I did by working longer and harder than anyone at my office. I looked at team members and employees who prioritized their families and outside interests critically; were they truly dedicated to our business success? Looking back, I can see that as far as my energy was concerned, I overcorrected. The irony is that during this period, I didn't come close to realizing my own potential because I was working with one hand tied behind my back. I was working without my Tiger gifts of intuition and empathy.

Whether we realize it or not, we are trained to turn off (or at least minimize) our Tiger energy while we work. We are trained to avoid showing emotion or getting too attached to any project or person, and we are told to stop taking everything so personally. We hear time and time again, "It's not personal, it's business." And yet, what could be more personal than our career? What could be more personal than our livelihood, the fruits of our daily efforts, our health insurance, and our relationships with the colleagues we interact with 2,000 hours a year? Honing our ability to be intuitive and empathetic is arguably just as critical as any other technical skill we acquire. Yet only a small amount of our training or school curriculum prepares us for how to *feel* more to *achieve* more.

Consider Profits, Not Just People

You might not be highly motivated by money, but the fact of the matter is that businesses need to make money. Put another way, all the love and connection in the world won't keep you in a career if the venture isn't profitable. Even if you work for a nonprofit or NGO, you are still part of a funded venture, so it's important that you understand the big picture, where you fit, and how you add value to the business. You need to take the time to work out your personal return on investment (ROI) and keep that in mind as you go about your day.

Balancing a love for people and pleasure with financial returns will ensure that you remain deeply valued. By all means, be about people, work as a team, collaborate, and have fun, but find the balance between the people, purpose, and profitability of the venture. And while you continue to remain in tune with the lives and feelings of those around you, keep in mind that your workplace Dragons are likely not operating on this same frequency. Try to not take it personally if your attempts to make a connection with those Dragons are ignored—they are just focused on a mission! Instead, seek out those around you who feed your energy. Find a work friend who will help you enjoy your day and give you the love that you need as you pursue your ROI. You really can have it all: a connection *and* career success.

If you are a Tiger leader, your strength is that you are more likely to invest the time and resources to coach and develop your team. Upon understanding motivators, you will then do what you can to help your people achieve their objectives. Remember, like you, your people need to perform and deliver their ROI, so be careful not to get too emotionally invested and involved in their personal lives. There is a balance that must be struck, and sometimes Tiger leaders cannot see the forest for the trees—so step back and try to see the entire ecosystem.

When you take a step back, you will also see that different people require different environments to thrive. You can't always motivate a Dragon with a carrot; instead you need to learn when to apply a little pressure to help your Dragons thrive. . . .

Tigers Love Pleasure; Pressure, Not So Much

Tigers look at pressure very differently from Dragons. Tiger energy expands, so work pressure can feel like one more layer to add to their existing pile of pressure. Work pressure gets added to home pressure, relationship pressure, health and fitness pressure. . . . Just throw it on the pile! All that pressure can become too much, at which point the Tiger becomes stressed out, which can then cause a Tiger to *react* emotionally rather than *act* productively. After all, Tigers prefer to work under *pleasure* rather than *pressure*, having the space and time to enjoy their job/craft and find their flow.

You can usually spot the dominant Tigers around the workplace—they are the ones having the most fun during the day. Tigers will tend to have a "best friend" at their workplace and will be the ones organizing and pushing for team lunches, group brainstorming meetings, and off-site team-building events. Dragons, on the other hand, don't get overly excited about the pleasure-filled office antics; they'd rather get on with the work and get it done. While Dragons don't mind having a laugh, Dragons don't need pleasure to perform.

You can't be safe and carefree all of the time. Life just doesn't work like that. But when you are feeling under pressure, overwhelmed, or unsafe, try to focus on what you can control; try to *act* rather than *react*. When you react, you push even deeper into your Tiger, so instead try to pull back a little and start to do what needs to be done.

If the pressure doesn't ease, you may need to decide if the current career or culture is going to be sustainable for your energy. If you find yourself constantly stressed and unhappy, you may want to do something different, because in the long term, if you are not happy and in your flow for the majority of the time, you won't perform at your best.

Meanwhile, if you are a Tiger leader and have a Tiger on your team who is not responding well to organizational pressure, try to understand how the Tiger is feeling and see if there is a way to relieve some of that pressure (whether temporarily or permanently). It may be that they need to vent and decompress, or they may need a day off to solve a nonwork-related matter that is pushing them over the edge. Check the last time they took their vacation—you may be surprised at how long it's been.

It is also important to keep in mind that your Dragon teammates need and enjoy a little pressure. You may struggle to retain talented Dragons if you don't give them a chance to test their limits. Dragons want to be pushed, and they like a little fear. So give them what they need to perform at their best.

Negotiating Your Worth

When it comes to negotiation, Tigers will try to anticipate the best outcome for everyone and will then be happy that everyone is happy (or at least equally unhappy). Even when I was deeply into my Dragon mode at work, for some reason I immediately moved into my Tiger energy whenever I entered into negotiations. And not just a little "toe dip in my Tiger," but I mean a full thrust into my Tiger energy—there was hardly even a whiff of my inner Dragon. I become overly empathetic, and I lose all focus on money/profits. I deeply fear the conflict, and it takes all of my energy to stand firm and not run away. This was such a strange feeling when I was so comfortable in my Dragon at work.

If a staff member would ask me for a pay rise, I would give it almost immediately. Even if that meant that our payroll ratios started to eat into our bottom line. I struggled to negotiate discounts with vendors, even if we received shoddy services. My team would look at me with absolute tilted heads, confused. "Who is she? Where is Gillian?"

I don't want to make it sound as if Tigers are inherently bad at negotiation. Tigers have naturally good intuition, which is very useful during negotiations because it enables them to be considerate and collaborative and work out what both parties want—and then they'll do their darndest to get to a place where everyone is happy.

However, as I found, when it comes to negotiations, particularly for your own worth, sometimes you have to lean into that Dragon energy to push your agenda forward. If you simply sit back and wait to be appreciated, recognized, or rewarded, you may be waiting for some time.

Keep in mind that having to fight for more money doesn't mean you aren't valued for all that you do. You may think some version of "*If you really saw my contribution and valued it, if you loved having me here, you would just volunteer more compensation. I shouldn't need to ask.*" But business doesn't often work like that. Sometimes you have to ask; sometimes you have to fight for it. Furthermore, don't be scared to ask for your worth because a higher salary could lead to equally higher expectations, which can feel like more pressure and less safety (and Tigers love to feel safe). Fight through your fear. You're stronger than you realize.

If you are a Tiger leader, don't feel obligated to give your Dragon employees everything they ask for (like me!). Dragons are purpose-driven and will go after their edge of potential. Take the time to understand their goals, help provide a pathway for them to achieve their missions, and compensate them fairly. Alternatively, when it comes to your Tiger employees, even if they might settle for words of encouragement, make sure you pay them their dues. Because those underpaid (yet highly appreciated) Tigers will be more inclined to leave than to uncomfortably keep incrementally asking you for more.

Finally, if you are scorned during negotiations, it may be hard for you to feel that you can trust that partner in the future or feel safe to negotiate with them again. Tigers tend to remember, whereas Dragons tend to forget. And when Tigers are negotiating with each other and negotiations fail, Tigers tend to burn all the bridges for the future. Try your best not to take it personally so you can keep the door open. You never know what is around the corner.

Recognizing the Value in Tiger Energy

For years, I was quick to discount the value of Tiger energy in the workplace, in part because I was socialized to value my Dragon "doing" over my Tiger "feeling." Luckily, my attitude changed, and I hope you Tigers out there will also recognize that the energy we bring to the workplace can play a critical role in creating a work environment that is fun, productive, people-centric, and profitable. And if you can use your Tiger gifts to continue to bring pleasure to the workplace even in times of high pressure, you'll be amazed at how successful you can be.

Coping with Opposite Energies at Work

The workplace is an environment that tends to affect our Dominant Energy on the daily, whether that means intentionally leaning more into your Dragon or your Tiger for optimal performance or unintentionally being pushed into a different energy by coworkers or culture. Here are a few takeaways to assist you in adjusting your energy in the workplace:

DRAGONS

- Try to relax into your Tiger a little from time to time, because finding the balance between achieving your purpose and connecting with people is important. Have some fun, and connect with those around you.

- When (and if) your workplace is pressure-fueled, pay attention to the energy of your coworkers and try to avoid being pulled into the emotional drama. Even the strongest Dragons can sometimes get lured into the Tiger chaos. Stay on mission, go deep into your Dragon energy, and remember your purpose.

- If there isn't a great deal of pressure in your workplace, you might find yourself feeling bored, restless, and unmotivated. In that work environment, you may need to create your own internal pressure to push yourself to your edge. Don't be afraid to bring in outside resources like a coach to help.

- Try not to get caught up in the competitive thrill of negotiating and lose sight of your desired outcome.

TIGERS

- It is important that you take the time to work out your personal ROI and keep that in mind as you go about your day. Find a balance between your desire for fun and connection with the purpose of the business (and financial returns).

- When you are feeling stressed or under pressure at work, try to focus on what you can control—try to "act" rather than "react."

- As a Tiger leader, you need to keep in mind that your Dragon teammates actually perform well under pressure. In order to retain talented Dragons, find ways to push them and give them the opportunity to find their edge of potential.

- From time to time, you will need to put yourself first, fight for yourself, and even fight for the best outcome for the business. We all have an inner Dragon, and there is a time and place to let it out. The negotiating table is that place.

Start Living in Polarity

All right, my Dragons and Tigers, it's time for you to go out into the wild and try putting some of these insights into action.

I suspect you've probably already started looking at people a little differently. Once I understood the power of Polarity, I started to see everyone in my life through an energetic lens. And when I started to see everyone around me as Tigers and Dragons, I couldn't unsee it.

If you haven't yet begun, I encourage you to be curious and start to mindfully contemplate the Dominant Energy of people in your orbit. When you spend time with your partner, friends, family, or colleagues, think back to Part I and consider whether they . . .

- Crave *freedom* (Dragon) over *being seen and loved* (Tiger)
- Prioritize their *missions* (Dragon) or their *relationships* (Tiger)
- Derive their pleasure from *competition* (Dragon) or *connection* (Tiger)

By being more mindful of the energy of those around us, we can start to better understand—and affect—our interactions. If someone is a Dragon, you can feed them with your respect, help them with their purpose, and engage in a little healthy competition. If someone is a Tiger, you can help them fill up with love, encourage them to feel, open your heart to them, and focus on connecting. All of this will have the effect of reducing conflict and fortifying your bonds with those close to you.

Keep in mind, of course, that the most important person to feed with respect or fill with love is your partner. You can have great energy with your colleagues, friends, and family, but let's be honest: To feel satisfied and fulfilled in the long haul, your primary relationship needs to be strong. This is the person you have chosen to walk through life with. And they're the one who, if you're committed to monogamy, you most want to have the biggest spark with.

If, as you read this book, you implemented its advice along the way, that spark is hopefully a roaring fire by now. However, if you're like most of us, you read the book front to back, thinking, "Once I understand, I'll do. Once I finish the book, I'll be ready." Well. Here you are. You're at the end. It's time to get going!

Start Doing the Work

It only takes one partner to consciously shift their energy to create the space for attraction. If you're reading this book, it will probably be you.

After everything Peter and I went through, I was the one to start practicing Polarity in our relationship. Peter was on board, but I had to initiate—over and over and over again. It wasn't easy and, certainly at first, it wasn't natural. As with any skill that requires practice—be it meditation, running, or playing the piano—I didn't always feel like it, but I knew it had to be done. In short, it was work.

As I wrote this book, I shared chapters with Peter along the way. After reading Part IV, Peter looked a little deflated. "Wow," he said. "I thought this change in our relationship was all just very natural and beautiful. I thought our love was so strong that it carried us through. But now that I am reading this, it's clear that this has all been 'work' for you." In some ways, he was right. At first it was a conscious effort; I really had to try, and that meant doing it when I didn't feel like it. Now, however, it has become such an important and positive part of our relationship that feeding him with respect and devotion is effortless and easy. Yet to get to this point, I had to put in the work. I had to start the process.

Someone has to start. So suck it up, and start to put in the work. Whether you are single or in a relationship, I challenge you to focus on feeding your Dominant Energy and consciously owning your inner Tiger or Dragon for the next thirty days. Try to do something every single day that feeds your Dominant Energy. Here are a few ideas to get you started:

DRAGONS

- Meditate for five minutes each day. While you are meditating, focus on pushing down and grounding yourself into the earth. Be the riverbed.

- Do something for one hour each day that moves you toward your purpose.

- Enter a competition and train for it. Maybe it's chess, a marathon, CrossFit, whatever—put yourself in a competitive environment.

- Plan a coffee/wine/dinner/walk with another Dragon whom you deeply respect.

TIGERS

- Meditate for five minutes each day. While you are meditating, focus on opening your heart. Breathe into your heart and release love back out into the world. Practice opening your heart each day.

- Do something each day that brings you an immense feeling of pleasure. Take a walk, chat with a friend, buy a bunch of flowers, eat a steak. . . . Whatever it is, acknowledge the pleasure before, during, and after the activity. Use that activity to fill up.

- Take time to surrender, even if it's just for an hour a week. Don't plan anything during that time, and be open to going where the moment takes you.

- Write a note to a friend or family member, someone whom you love and care about. Write something that you know will make their heart swell with love. Then seal it up and mail it. (Yep, with a stamp.)

Feed Your Relationship Polarity

If you are in a relationship, I challenge you to go one step further and, in addition to feeding your own energy, start to make a conscious effort to improve your Polarity. Try to do something every day that feeds your partner's Dominant Energy. Create some space!

If you're a Dragon, you can start to feed your partner doses of love and attention while you practice standing firm and holding space for them. Here are some ideas you can try to encourage your partner's Tiger energy:

- Run a bath and lead your Tiger there at the end of the day.

- Pay attention to what brings your Tiger pleasure, and make a list. It might be yoga, a bunch of flowers, walking the dog, or talking to friends. Lead your Tiger to that pleasure each day. Ensure your Tiger has time and space to really bask in their pleasure. And when they do, be sure to tell them how glorious they look when they are happy.

- Do something to activate your Tiger's senses (in a good way!). Wear a new perfume or cologne, light a scented candle, cook something fragrant, watch a sunset together, take a moment to listen to the leaves dropping during fall, play a fun song and dance together, take off your shoes and go together for a walk around the yard on the cold grass. . . . The possibilities are endless.

- Take your partner away for the weekend or out for the evening. When you do, make sure you plan *everything*. Be meticulous. Plan like it's a work assignment. Then, during your time away, don't waver from your resolve. Lead your partner through the weekend. If your partner criticizes your choices (which they will), let those criticisms roll off your sturdy Dragon shoulders.

If you're a Tiger, you can start to feed your partner with large doses of respect and practice surrendering to them while opening your heart to your own pleasure. Here are some suggestions to encourage your partner's Dragon energy:

- Send your partner a text or a voice recording where you tell them how and why you are proud of them. Describe

something they do really well and how you respect
them for that, and maybe even how sexy it is to you.

- The next time you are out at a dinner or event, publicly
recognize your partner for doing something great. Lay it
on thick, and be earnest.

- Surrender decision-making. Let your partner choose
the movie, the restaurant, and even the song playing in
the car. Don't criticize their decision; instead, tell them
how nice it is when they take the lead.

- Organize a dinner or outing with someone you know
your partner admires and respects.

Practice, Practice, Practice

Keep a journal of what you do each day, and make note of any
changes in yourself, as well as your relationship. How are you feeling? Is there more desire and attraction? Is your partner behaving
differently? Keep notes as the month progresses.

At the end of the month, take a moment to look back over your
notes and contemplate your energetic evolution. If you put in
the work, I know you will already be seeing and feeling changes.
You will start to feel more authentic and more centered. You will
start to notice people looking at you differently, even more desir-
ably, particularly your partner. If you aren't yet seeing or feeling
a change, I encourage you to stick with it. It can take time to fully
embody your Tiger or Dragon (especially when you're deep in
the opposite energy, the way I was with my Dragon!).

Once you are feeling and seeing a change in your relationship,
you will be motivated to keep going. Commit to another thirty days.

Then do it again. Before you know it, you won't even have to try. You will be instinctively living your life in your Dominant Energy, and your relationship will be experiencing such natural and beautiful Polarity it will be hard to remember what your life was like before.

I also encourage you to do an energetic "check-in" every month and journal how you are feeling. Meditate to reflect on whether you are feeding your Dominant Energy or if you have slipped back into old habits. If you feel yourself slipping, come back to this book and refresh yourself by rereading your favorite passages or chapters. Remember the power and importance of pleasure and passion in your life!

Reframing: Differences Are a Gift, Not a Torment

An important tool in the Polarity toolbox is *reframing*. Specifically, this is reframing the differences between ourselves and our partner as gifts to each other, rather than sources of torment. When we are different from our partner, the temptation is to view them as a slightly worse version of ourselves. We need to stop doing that.

For the longest time I couldn't see my Tiger ability to multitask as a gift; I saw multitasking as normal and Peter's inability to multitask as his shortcoming. The resentment was awful. I felt as if I had to do it all: I had to work, feed our family, take primary responsibility for the kids' schooling, their pediatrician visits, their trips to the dentist, their social calendars (and all the bloody birthday presents). . . . The weight of the household was on my shoulders. I even had to call the pest control guy. Taking on all that responsibility weighed down my head and my heart. Peter, on the other hand, would simply put one foot in front of the other until he ran into something. He'd get up, go to work, and then worry about home when he got home. If he returned home and there was no food in the fridge, he simply ordered some, because he hadn't thought about it before that moment. I didn't know how he could do that. It was *so frustrating!*

When I shared my frustrations with my Tiger friends, they would say the exact same thing about their Dragon partners. We would share our war stories and get each other all riled up. Then I learned to reframe, and everything changed.

"Doing it all" is my gift that I can give to Peter (and to our girls). I have a special ability to multitask. I have the innate fluidity that allows me to hold many ideas in my mind and many people in my heart all at once. And through that beautiful, natural gift, I have the ability to nurture and nourish my family. If Peter had that ability, he would do it, too. But he doesn't. He can't hold all of that at once. I bring that ability to him and my family and friends, and it fills me with joy. What a gift to be able to care for them like that!

Peter's gift to me is that his inner Dragon energy operates linearly. He is able to apply singular focus to his career and business, and as a result he is very successful. Then, when he brings his deep consciousness and presence to me and takes the Dragon Throne, it soothes me, snaps me back to the moment, and helps ground me in the here and now. When he is here in the moment with me, he is fully present.

While I hold *everything,* he holds *me.* That is our gift to each other. And when you are able to reframe your energy and your partner's energy as gifts, you too will feel resentment and tension melt away.

I encourage you to write down in your journal the gifts you and your partner offer each other. What does your partner do well that you can't? What do you do well that your partner can't? If you work at this, you will uncover all of the attractive, sexy, beautiful, different things that you offer each other.

Of course, that's not to say you won't ever feel frustrated again. In those moments, try to write down what it is that's bothering you about your partner. Could that frustration be reframed? Are you really just frustrated by a difference in your energetic approach to life?

Your partner is different from you and that is a good thing!

Coming Full Circle

I started this book with a disclosure that few people in my life (let alone the public) know about. And despite all the time it has taken me to write and release this book, I continue to have anxiety about sharing my story. In particular, I am concerned for our daughters. When they read these pages, will they see their father differently? Negatively? Will they judge me for staying in the marriage? Or will they respect the hard work we've put in to reclaim the gift that is our marriage and family?

Through these pages, I hope they can come to the same realization that you have hopefully made: We can go beyond merely surviving trauma and use the moments of deepest heartbreak to evolve. These are opportunities to go deeper into our consciousness and peel back the layers to reveal more of ourselves. And as impossible as it may seem, if we take healing one day at a time and remain attentive and committed to our growth, we can lead rewarding lives brimming with respect, purpose, passion, and pleasure. By closely observing ourselves and our energy, by caring deeply and devoting ourselves to our own evolution and to the evolution of our relationships, we can keep love, longing, and even lust alive.

It is with pride that I can say that my first marriage to Peter is officially over. During our first seventeen years together, we shared some beautiful moments, but looking back, I see those scenes are littered with lies, conflict, trauma, and shame. And for the most part, that marriage was devoid of passion.

Today we have a completely new, healthy, and (mostly) happy relationship. Despite the deep pain Peter and I caused each other, we have been able to hold on to our friendship, family, and financial security while also rekindling the desire that brought us together in the first place. Don't get me wrong: We are far from perfect. We still go to therapy once or twice a month, we still argue, and there are still times when Peter frustrates the hell out of me (and, I'm sure, vice versa), but those are now the exceptions rather than the norm.

In my eyes, Peter is now an awe-inspiring, grounded, purpose-driven Dragon. He is living his life to his fullest potential. And through his energetic depth and strength, he holds me and keeps me feeling safe enough to let go into my sparkling, open, pleasure-loving Tiger.

Peter feels respected, and I feel seen and loved—and *that* is a beautiful thing. That is the power of Polarity.

Acknowledgments

Firstly, there is no way this book could have been written without the exceptional coaching and editing of Allison Goldstein. Thank you for asking the hard questions and dragging me into a modern vernacular.

I want to acknowledge the brilliant and insightful modern-day gurus whose works deeply inspired these pages: Regena Thomashauer, John Wineland, and David Deida. I want to especially thank Jenna Harper for introducing me to their work and starting me on this path to healing. You are a true lightworker.

Thank you to all of the family and friends who have generously shared their lives in these pages....

To my inner support circle who shared in my pain and carried me through my very darkest of days: Mum, Libby, Tony, Miranda, Shona, and Lauren—I love you beyond words.

Finally, thank you to Peter Harper for wholeheartedly supporting this book and my current life path. Thank you for allowing me to share our story with the world—I know it won't be easy, but I also know we can handle it together. Thank you for evolving with me. Thank you for loving me. Thank you for being my Dragon.

About the Author

Gillian Harper is an author, speaker, coach, and entrepreneur. Gillian helped build Australia's number one franchise, served as an executive for a US Inc. 500 business, and has practiced as a finance attorney with an Australian top three firm. Gillian has also been an international speaker and coach for more than twenty years, observing and coaching hundreds of business owners through the daily challenges of entrepreneurship.

Gillian knows firsthand that the boundaries that divide our careers and our home life are blurred. And one thing is for certain: It is hard to reach your potential without a solid foundation.

After her own foundation crumbled and she almost lost everything, Gillian became a devout student of all things energy. She became enamored with the ancient Egyptian teachings of *The Kybalion*, enlightened by the Taoist way, and fascinated by Kundalini yoga and Vajrayana practices. Finally, she discovered what she was looking for: the little-known Law of Polarity that brought her life back from the brink.

Gillian has made it her mission to share her insights and continue her work helping others. By combining her knowledge of

Polarity with her business and coaching acumen, Gillian has developed an energy-fueled system to assist you to create and maintain a more powerful, passionate, and fulfilling existence.